Turkish Culture for Americans

by

(in alphabetical order)

Hasan Dindi
Maija Gazur
Wayne M. Gazur
Ayşen Kırkköprü–Dindi

First Edition

1989

International Concepts, Ltd.

Boulder, Colorado, U.S.A.

Published by International Concepts, Ltd.
5311 Holmes Place, Boulder, CO 80303–1243, U.S.A.

Library of Congress Cataloging-in-Publication Data

Dindi, Hasan; Gazur, Maija; Gazur, Wayne M.; and Kırkköprü–Dindi,
Ayşen
    Turkish Culture for Americans

    Includes bibliography.
    1. Intercultural communication–Turkey. 2. Turkish Culture.
    3. Culture Assimilator. 4. Cross-cultural studies–Turkey. I. Title.
Library of Congress Catalog Card Number   88–083130
ISBN 0–924602–44–9

First Printing, May 1989

ACKNOWLEDGEMENTS

We sincerely thank the following people for their assistance. This book would not have been possible without their generous support.

Barbara Ayre

Robert Ayre

Mike Burns

Peggy Burns

Gökhan Danabaşoğlu

Meftun Erdoğan

Joan Eröncel

Joel Fisher

Lija Fisher

Ann Gazur

Helen J. Gazur

Michael J. Gazur

Hatice Geçol

Mary Ann Goff

William J. Griswold

Cezmi Kuru

Helen Irene MacConnell

Donald C. Martin

Karen A. Martin

Ceyhun Ortancıl

Kenan Özekin

Zaiga Siktars

Harry C. Triandis

Michael F. Tucker

Marlies West

Ron West

Janet Wolney

Richard Wolney

We also thank the International Division of Moran, Stahl, & Boyer for their encouragement and support.

ABOUT THE AUTHORS

Hasan Dindi is a research associate in the Center for Combustion Research at the University of Colorado at Boulder. He holds a B.S. Degree from İstanbul Technical University, and M.S. and Ph.D. Degrees from the University of Colorado at Boulder, all in Chemical Engineering. His areas of interest include synfuels technology development, petroleum processing and combustion fluid mechanics. During the past five years he has been involved in the cross-cultural training of Americans leaving for business assignments in Turkey. Mr. Dindi enjoys playing and officiating soccer, and using personal computers.

Maija Gazur had her first introduction to cross-cultural issues at the age of two when she and her family fled Latvia to live in displaced persons camps in Austria. They immigrated to the United States in 1951. Her involvement with Turkey began in 1966 as a Peace Corps Volunteer in Samsun. Later she returned to Turkey and taught at Robert College in İstanbul, where both of her children were born. Ms. Gazur has a M.A. Degree in Counseling. She is a cross-cultural consultant to Moran, Stahl, & Boyer and trains American business people departing for foreign countries, including Turkey. She enjoys skiing, bicycling, and travel.

Wayne M. Gazur is a lecturer at the University of Colorado at Boulder, teaching in an interdisciplinary program between the College of Business and Administration and the School of Law. He holds a B.S. Degree in Accounting from the University of Wyoming, a Juris Doctor Degree from the University of Colorado at Boulder, and a Master of Laws in Taxation from the University of Denver. His areas of specialization include taxation and business planning. Prior to entering teaching, Mr. Gazur practiced as an attorney and before that as a Certified Public Accountant. His hobbies include bicycling and skiing.

Ayşen Kırkköprü–Dindi is a Ph.D. candidate in the Department of Chemical Engineering at the University of Colorado at Boulder. She holds a B.S. Degree from İstanbul Technical University, and a M.S. Degree from the University of Colorado at Boulder, both in Chemical Engineering. Her research areas include coal processing and membrane technology. During the past five years, as a consultant, she has participated in the cross-cultural and Turkish language training of American business people departing for Turkey. She enjoys aerobics and jogging.

Table of Contents

PREFACE

The purpose of this book is to help Americans understand the basics of Turkish culture. This is accomplished by the presentation of 73 cross-cultural episodes involving interactions between Americans and Turks. In addition, since a culture is woven with threads such as geography, history, religion, language, and values, the book also includes some introductory information of this nature.

This book is the product of a combination of several factors, some practical, some theoretical, and some social. From the practical standpoint, the authors noted that in spite of the opening of Turkey to international business in 1980, there was a lack of information concerning American/Turkish cultural interaction. From the theoretical standpoint, current research in the cross-cultural area indicated that an effective means of changing people's attitudes with respect to a given culture was through the use of an instrument called a "culture assimilator." This format utilized a series of cross-cultural episodes demonstrating a cultural misunderstanding between people from two different cultures. From the social standpoint, the authors met one another in 1985 and discovered their common interest in Turkey. The Turkish authors (HD & AK-D) came to the States for graduate studies. One of the American authors (MG) had lived in Turkey for five years, and both of her children were born during her stay in İstanbul. The fourth author (WMG) offered an American's perspective to the project. As with most creative endeavors, the spark of inspiration was required. That spark was provided to one of the authors (MG) while Nordic skiing on the brisk, sunny, Christmas Eve Day of 1987, when the whole project was conceived.

The book consists of four sections. The first section provides general background information about Turkey. The second section consists of a practical guide to the Turkish language. The third section contains a comparison of differing American and Turkish cultural values. The fourth section presents 73 cross-cultural episodes, each of which illustrates a Turkish cultural point which may be confusing to Americans.

The suggestions presented in this book are generalizations of individual behaviors. One of the potential pitfalls of such generalizations is that it may cause people to stereotype. Hence the suggestions given in this book are intended only as general guidelines
and not as concrete absolutes for dealing with specific individuals.

This book should be considered a part of a continuing process. It
will undoubtedly be refined through the feedback of readers. Additional cultural observations of Americans in Turkey will be an
important resource in furthering this process. The authors therefore encourage the submission of such information and comments
to the publisher. Please use the form provided at the end of the
book for this purpose.

H.D., M.G., W.M.G. and A.K–D.

May, 1989
Boulder, Colorado, U.S.A.

I.
A VIEW OF TURKEY

Turkey is a social, cultural, as well as a geographical bridge, between Europe and Asia. Consequently, one can find westernized Turks who speak excellent English as well as Turks who have never left their village. All of the diverse groups that comprise Turkish society, however, share a deep pride in their Turkish roots and traditions. The hospitality of Turkish people toward guests, for example, is one of those traditions.

The purpose of this section is to briefly acquaint the reader with some basic facts about Turkey.

A. Geography

Turkey's area is approximately 302,000 square miles, which is slightly larger than the state of Texas. The Asian part of Turkey, known as Anatolia or Asia Minor, comprises 97 percent of Turkey's land mass and is technically a peninsula, rectangular in shape, lying between the Mediterranean Sea to the south and the Black Sea to the north. The European part is sometimes called Thrace and represents only a small portion (3 percent), of the country's land mass. The European and Asian parts are separated by the Sea of Marmara which lies between the Black Sea on the east, and the Aegean Sea on the west. The Sea of Marmara meets the Black Sea at İstanbul where the European and Asian land masses are separated by the Bosphorus Strait. The Sea of Marmara again narrows on the western side to meet the Aegean Sea at Çanakkale, at a strait called the Dardanelles.

As shown by the map on the following page, Turkey is bordered by six countries: Greece and Bulgaria to the northwest, the Soviet Union and Iran on the east, and Iraq and Syria on the south.

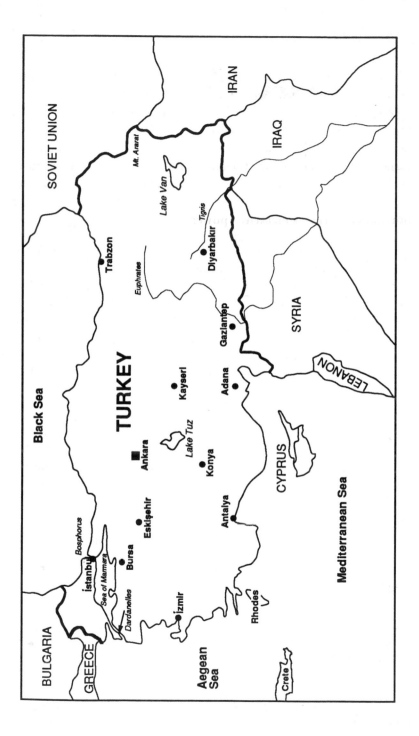

The eastern part of Turkey is in large part a high plateau, punc-
tuated by mountains. Mount Ararat (Ağrı Dağı), thought to be
where Noah's Ark landed, is located near the Soviet border, and
is the highest mountain in Turkey, reaching 16,946 feet. There
are a number of lakes and rivers in Anatolia (Lake Van being the
largest). The Tigris (Dicle) and Euphrates (Fırat) rivers have
their sources in the mountains and highlands of eastern Anatolia,
and hydroelectric dams built on these rivers provide a significant
portion of Turkey's electrical power.

Turkey has three climatic regions which display different weather
conditions. The areas which border the Black Sea enjoy a tem-
perate climate with a significant amount of rainfall. The Mediterranean, Aegean and Sea of Marmara regions enjoy a Mediterranean climate which is a little warmer and drier than the Black
Sea areas to the north. The central and eastern Anatolian regions
are marked by cold winters and hot, dry summers.

Average Temperatures at Selected Weather Stations
(All temperatures are in degrees Fahrenheit)[1]

	Marmara (İstanbul)	Aegean (İzmir)	Mediter. (Antalya)	C. Anat. (Ankara)	Black Sea (Trabzon)	E. Anat. (Van)
Jan.	41	48	50	32	45	28
Feb.	43	50	52	34	45	28
March	45	52	55	41	46	32
April	54	61	61	52	54	41
May	63	68	68	61	61	54
June	70	77	77	68	68	61
July	75	82	82	73	73	68
Aug.	75	81	82	73	73	66
Sept.	68	73	77	64	68	57
Oct.	59	64	68	55	61	45
Nov.	54	57	59	46	55	36
Dec.	46	50	54	36	50	31

[1]Source: Turkey in Brief, Turkish Embassy Culture and Tourism Counselor's Office

At the time of the 1985 census, Turkey's population was 51 million (estimated at 55 million in 1988). The population continues
to grow at the rate of approximately 2.5 percent annually. Although there is a strong trend toward urbanization, over half of
the population lives in rural areas or small towns. The population
of the major cities according to the 1985 census is: İstanbul (5.5
million), Ankara, the capital, (2.5 million), İzmir (1.5 million),
Adana (776,000) and Bursa (650,000).

B. History

Turkey lies to the west of the region once known as Mesopotamia,
the "Cradle of Civilization." As a consequence, a number of civ-
ilizations played roles in Turkey's long and rich history. Of the
more ancient peoples, the Hittites were the most significant in
the years beginning with approximately 2,000 B.C. Turkey was
the site of the ten-year Trojan War in the years around 1200
B.C. In approximately 550 B.C. the Persians established rule
over much of Anatolia, falling to Alexander the Great in 334 B.C.
From about 100 B.C. to the 11th century, Romans ruled much of
Turkey. In 330 A.D. the Roman emperor Constantine designated
Constantinople (now İstanbul) as the capital of the Eastern Roman Empire, which later became known as the Byzantine Empire.
The Byzantine Empire started to decline after the end of Emperor
Justinian's reign in 565, and the following years saw Islamic in-
roads against Byzantine rule. In the 11th century the Seljuk Turks
arrived from Central Asia. They had embraced Islam, and their
arrival signaled the beginning of the Turkification of the region.
The defeat of the Byzantine army in 1071 at the Battle of Manzik-
ert (Malazgirt Savaşı) established Seljuk control in Anatolia. The
"Ottoman Empire" was established in the 13th century by Osman Bey, the leader of a Seljuk tribe. Ottoman power was firmly
established by the fall of Constantinople in 1453. One of the
most famous Ottoman rulers was Süleyman "The Magnificent"
(also known as "The Lawgiver"), who ruled from 1520 to 1566.
Süleyman's empire spanned over 8 million square miles, stretching
from Vienna to the Arabian peninsula. The Empire in part owed

the successful governance of its territories to a well-organized system of government and a policy of religious tolerance.

During the 17th and 18th centuries, the Ottoman power declined in the face of growing nationalism in the Ottoman territories, and parts of the Empire were lost. In the 19th century, the list of lost possessions included Moldavia, Romania, and southern Greece.

The late 19th and early 20th centuries were a time of political unrest in the lands of the Ottoman Empire. Under the direction of the "Young Turks", who controlled the government during the decade preceding the war, the Ottoman Empire fought in World War I against the Allies. After the war an armistice was signed, but the allied forces occupied most of Anatolia. Mustafa Kemal, the victorious leader of the Turkish forces at the battle of Gallipoli, started a military and political campaign in Anatolia to avoid the dismemberment of Turkey at the hands of the victorious Allies. After years of warfare, marked by various treaties, a number of foreign forces, Greeks, British, Italians, and French were driven from Anatolia, and modern Turkey was born. By the Treaty of Lausanne on July 24, 1923, today's borders (with some minor exceptions) were confirmed. A republic was proclaimed on October 29, 1923, and Ankara became the capital. After the Turkish War of Independence, Turkey turned toward modernization. The moving force was again Mustafa Kemal, known as Atatürk, "Father of the Turks." He is without question the most revered hero of modern Turkey.

Atatürk's main reforms were westernization and secularism. Earlier leaders such as the Sultans were both political and religious functionaries (Caliphs). The Sultanate and the Caliphate were both abolished by Atatürk, in favor of a secular state. The Constitution was adopted to provide for freedom of religion, and Islam assumed a religious, but non-political, role. The wearing of the fez or turban was outlawed for men and the veil for women. A civil code, modeled after Swiss law, was adopted. The Gregorian calendar replaced the Islamic lunar calendar. The Metric system was adopted. The Latin alphabet replaced Arabic script. Women were given the right to vote.

Turks are very proud of their national heritage. Atatürk is held in very high regard, his picture appearing in almost every shop, government building and public place. Everyone is expected to show respect to the national anthem, the flag, and the memory of Atatürk. Turks are also very proud and protective of their rich history. Due in large part to the theft of many of Turkey's treasures by archeologists and others from foreign countries in the past, Turkey has enacted very strict laws prohibiting the possession or export of antiquities, and these laws prescribe severe penalties. The term "antiquity" is broadly construed and can include items such as carpets.

After Atatürk's death on November 10, 1938, Turkey continued to concentrate on its internal development. Turkey remained neutral during most of World War II. The postwar years were marked by political and social strife with several military coups, the last occurring in 1980. Elections were held in 1983, and political stability has prevailed. Turkey has been an important member of NATO since 1952, and the most dependable ally of the United States in the Middle East. Turkish troops fought bravely in the Korean conflict with the United States and other United Nations forces.

C. Economy

The Turkish economy has one of the fastest growth rates in the world. In 1986 and 1987 the growth rates were 8 percent and 7.5 percent, respectively. A consequence of this rapid growth has been a high rate of inflation. A factor contributing to the economic difficulties experienced by Turkey in the last two decades is the fact that it imports 80 percent of its petroleum requirements and does not fit the stereotype of the oil rich Middle Eastern country. The agricultural sector remains important in terms of income and exports, and Turkey is a major producer of wheat and other grains and cereals. Manufacturing will play an increasingly important role in the future. Textile and clothing production are Turkey's most important manufacturing industries, followed by ceramics, steel and paper.

Historically, the State owned many of the largest industries in Turkey such as coal, textile, sugar and petroleum. In 1980 the government embarked on a plan to open the country to foreign investment and greater private competition. As part of the government's measures to encourage private competition, it started to privatize some of these industries. An important pending development is Turkey's admission to the European Economic Community (EEC) as a full member. Turkey has been an associate member of the EEC since 1963 and applied for full membership in April, 1987. Membership would open European markets to the products of Turkey's competitive agriculture and textile industries. On the other hand, some Turkish enterprises, such as the automotive and steel industries, would need to adapt to an environment lacking protective tariffs.

D. Government and Politics

Under the Turkish Constitution, legislative power is held by the Turkish Grand National Assembly, a unicameral body. Elections are held every five years. The President is elected by the Grand National Assembly for the period of seven years and is the Head of State, representing the nation and acting as the Commander in Chief of the armed forces. The President appoints the Prime Minister who exercises executive power as head of the Council of Ministers. The Turkish military is considered the guardian of the democracy. It has intervened in politics from time to time, the most recent occasion being in 1980 when a military coup replaced the government of Prime Minister Süleyman Demirel. General elections were then held in 1983 in which the government headed by Prime Minister Turgut Özal, was elected. Mr. Özal was re-elected in the elections held in 1987. The current President is Kenan Evren.

E. Religion

The vast majority (about 98 percent) of the Turkish population
is Moslem. The religion is Islam and the holy book is the Ko-
ran. However, Turkey is a secular state and freedom of religion
is guaranteed by the Constitution. Armenian, Greek, and Jewish
minorities follow their faiths in an atmosphere of tolerance. It is,
however, illegal to proselytize, to distribute religious literature, or
to otherwise engage in any such activity.

F. Holidays

Although Turkey follows the Gregorian calendar, religious holidays are determined according to the lunar calendar, and their
dates determined by the Gregorian calendar fall about ten days
earlier each year. The significant Turkish holidays are indicated
below.

- Ramazan Holiday or Candy Holiday (Ramazan Bayramı
  or Şeker Bayramı), A three-day holiday which follows Ramazan, the month of fasting.

- Feast of the Sacrifice Holiday (Kurban Bayramı), (a four-
  day holiday which falls 70 days after Ramazan Bayramı).

- New Year's Day (Yılbaşı), January 1.

- National Sovereignty and Children's Day (Milli Egemenlik
  ve Çocuk Bayramı), April 23.

- Atatürk Memorial and Youth and Sports Day (Atatürk'ü
  Anma ve Gençlik ve Spor Bayramı), May 19.

- Victory Day (Zafer Bayramı), August 30.

- Labor Day (İşçi Bayramı), September 1.

- Republic Day (Cumhuriyet Bayramı), October 29.

II.
SURVIVAL TURKISH

Knowledge of the language is an important factor in successfully adjusting to a new culture. The purpose of this section is to provide a practical introduction to the Turkish language.

A. Turkish Alphabet

LETTERS	APPROXIMATE PRONUNCIATION
A a	but, come
B b	beautiful, but
C c	jelly, Jim
Ç ç	church, cherry
D d	dear, dip
E e	red, bet
F f	fine, fake
G g	good, gate
Ğ ğ	weigh, sleigh
H h	hate, hell
I ı	wanted, syllable
İ i	skin, mint
J j	treasure, leisure
K k	kick, cast
L l	lucky, lazy
M m	money, machine
N n	never, narrow
O o	open, go
Ö ö	curve, serve
P p	peasant, pet
R r	root, riot
S s	seek, sea
Ş ş	sheriff, should
T t	take, talk
U u	root, book
Ü ü	tu, sur in French
V v	vest, vita
Y y	young, yes
Z z	zone, zero

B. Travel

TURKISH	ENGLISH
Türkiye	Turkey
Türkçe	Turkish (language)
Türk	Turk
Amerika	U.S.A.
Amerikalr	American
İngilizce	English
Araba	Car, cart
Otobüs	Bus
Vapur	Boat
Uçak	Airplane
Bilet	Ticket
Ne kadar?	How much?
Taksi	Taxi
Otobüs Durağı	Bus-stop
Havaalanı	Airport
Liman	Port
Ne?	What?
Nerede?	Where?
Nereden?	From where?

C. Introduction/Greetings

Merhaba.	Hello.
Selam.	Hi.
Hoş geldiniz.	Welcome.
Hoş bulduk.	"I am happy to be here," said in response to "Hoş geldiniz."
Nasılsınız?	How are you? (formal)
Nasılsın?	How are you? (informal)
İyiyim.	I am fine.
Ne var? Ne yok?	What is new?

İyilik, sağlık.	"All is well," said in response to "Ne var? Ne yok?"
Teşekkür ederim.	Thank you.
Tanıştırayım.	Let me introduce you.
Eşim.	My spouse.
Arkadaşım.	My friend.
Tanıştığımıza memnun oldum.	I am pleased to meet you.
Ben de memnun oldum.	I am pleased too.
Bey	Mr.
John (Smith) Bey	Mr. (John) Smith
Hanım	Ms.
Linda (Smith) Hanım	Ms. (Linda) Smith
Günaydın.	Good morning.
Tünaydın.	Good afternoon.
İyi akşamlar.	Good evening.
İyi geceler.	Good night.
İyi günler.	Have a good day.
Allahaısmarladık.	"Good bye," said by the person who leaves.
Güle güle.	"Good bye," said by the person who stays.
Affedersiniz.	Excuse me.
İngilizce biliyor musunuz?	Do you know English?
Anlamadım.	I do not understand.
Lütfen tekrar ediniz.	Please repeat it.
Evet	Yes
Hayır	No
Kayboldum.	I am lost.

D. Shopping

Pazar	Bazaar, market
Dükkan	Shop, store
Para	Money
Ucuz	Inexpensive
Pahalı	Expensive

Açık	Open
Kapalı	Closed
Çok	Much, large, many
Az	Little, small, few
İyi	Good
Kötü	Bad
Metre	Meter
Kilo	Kilogram
Kaç kilo?	How many kilograms?
Gram	Gram
Kaç gram?	How many grams?
Lira	Lira (Turkish money unit)
TL	Turkish Lira

E. Numbers

Bir	One
İki	Two
Üç	Three
Dört	Four
Beş	Five
Altı	Six
Yedi	Seven
Sekiz	Eight
Dokuz	Nine
On	Ten
Yirmi	Twenty
Otuz	Thirty
Kırk	Forty
Elli	Fifty
Altmış	Sixty
Yetmiş	Seventy
Seksen	Eighty
Doksan	Ninety
Yüz	One hundred
Bin	One thousand

Milyon	Million
Milyar	Billion
On bir	Eleven
Elli iki	Fifty-two
Sekiz yüz yirmi dokuz	Eight hundred twenty-nine
Yedi bin yüz yirmi altı	Seven thousand one hundred twenty-six

F. Colors

Beyaz	White
Siyah	Black
Mavi	Blue
Yeşil	Green
Kırmızı	Red
Sarı	Yellow
Turuncu	Orange
Mor	Purple
Pembe	Pink
Kahverengi	Brown
Gri	Grey

G. Days, Months, ...

Pazar	Sunday
Pazartesi	Monday
Salı	Tuesday
Çarşamba	Wednesday
Perşembe	Thursday
Cuma	Friday
Cumartesi	Saturday
Hafta	Week
Gün	Day
Ocak	January
Şubat	February

Mart	March
Nisan	April
Mayıs	May
Haziran	June
Temmuz	July
Ağustos	August
Eylül	September
Ekim	October
Kasım	November
Aralık	December
Ay	Month
Mevsim	Season
İlkbahar	Spring
Yaz	Summer
Sonbahar	Fall
Kış	Winter
Yıl	Year
23 Aralık 1988	December 23, 1988
23/12/1988	12/23/1988

H. Common Phrases

Çok yaşa.	"God bless you," or "Live long," said to a person who sneezes.
Sen de gör.	The equivalent of "Thank you," in this case. Said by the person who sneezes.
Maşallah.	"May God protect him/her/it from the evil eye."
İnşallah.	"If God wills," shows hope for a good event.
Kolay gelsin.	"Take it easy," said to a person who is working.
Geçmiş olsun.	"Get well soon," said to a person who is/was sick.

Başın sağolsun.	"Accept my condolences," expresses sympathy on the death of a person.
Ellerine sağlık.	Literally "Health to your hands." Usually said to the hostess in appreciation for a good meal.
Afiyet olsun.	"Good appetite," response to "Ellerine Sağlık."
Buyrun.	"Come on in," or "Go ahead."
Efendim.	"Sir" or "Pardon me."
Hayırlı işler.	"Have a good, profitable day," said to a shopkeeper.
Tebrik ederim.	"Congratulations."
Güle güle oturun.	Literally "May you live happily," said when someone moves to a new residence.
Sağol.	"Thank you."
Bir şey değil.	"Do not mention it," or "It is nothing," is response to "Teşekkür ederim."
Güle güle giy.	Literally "Wear it happily," said when someone has bought something new to wear.
Hayırlı yolculuklar.	"Have a good trip."
Bayramınız kutlu olsun.	"Have a happy holiday."
Doğum gününüz kutlu olsun.	"Happy Birthday."

III.
CONTRASTING THE VALUES

The purpose of this section is to present a framework for understanding Turkish culture. This will be accomplished by exploring some Turkish values that differ significantly from those held by most Americans.

Culture could be defined as the collection of commonly shared values, beliefs, behaviors, customs and other characteristics that earmark certain people as an original and distinct group. In understanding Turkish culture, it is helpful to interpret actions or behaviors as being based on certain values of the culture.

The following chart compares some of the significantly differing values of the American and Turkish cultures. The chart is followed by an explanation of each of the contrasting values.

U.S.A.	TURKEY
Time/Action	Interaction
Individualism	Group Affiliation
Goal Oriented	Being Oriented
Direct/Open	Indirect/Tactful
Disclosing	Face Saving/Honor
Informal	Formal
Assertive	Passive
Casual Friendships	Deep Friendships
Equality	Hierarchy
Competition	Cooperation
Optimistic	Faith/Fatalistic

A. Time/Action vs. Interaction

In general, American culture places great importance upon time, action and getting things done. Popular phrases such as "a mover and shaker" or "a man of action" carry very positive connotations.

Time is viewed as a valuable commodity to be saved and used wisely in achieving progress. Schedules, efficiency, and meeting deadlines are given great importance. People are expected to be punctual in arriving at scheduled events. This view, however, can result in neglect of personal relationships when it conflicts with "getting the job done."

On the other hand, in Turkish culture there is a more relaxed attitude toward time. Time is something that exists as a backdrop to human activity. Interaction with others is highly valued. Maintaining good relationships is emphasized. A Turk may view the American preoccupation with time as slavish and inhibiting one's enjoyment of life. This approach to time may be a source of much frustration for Americans. Turks, however, consider fostering relationships as an essential part of getting things accomplished. Schedules may be met more easily if the interaction aspect is taken into account, and appropriate allowances are made.

B. Individualism vs. Group Affiliation

The United States is generally considered to be a culture in which individualism is highly valued. Being "Number One" is a position eagerly sought. Children are reared to be independent and self-reliant; individual self-expression is encouraged. This value stresses autonomy and exercising initiative on one's own behalf. An American's sense of identity and self-esteem is defined according to his/her accomplishments. A common American belief is that anyone can be successful through hard work and persistence no matter how humble one's background. Membership in many groups is common, but the individual's identity and behavior are defined independently of the group. Individualism may manifest itself in materialism as well as pursuit of personal pleasure. Privacy is highly valued.

In Turkey, one belongs to a few groups, but group affiliation is very important. A Turk's identity is largely determined by the group, such as the family, school group or work group. Family attachments are very strong, including the extended family. An individual's behavior is expected to conform to the norms and traditions of the group. Turks consider the group's goals to be as important as their own. There is reliance on, trust of, and sharing among members of the group but mistrust of outsiders. Therefore the group is important because it provides protection from outsiders, and the in-group provides contacts to get things accomplished.

C. Goal Oriented vs. Being Oriented

Americans are goal and future oriented. Setting and achieving goals are driving forces in life, in a desire to make the future better than the past or present. Americans spend a great deal of time and money on self-improvement activities, such as education, athletics, and weight control programs. A sense of personal accomplishment and monetary gain are often the primary motivating factors.

Turks, on the other hand, are more people and relationship oriented. Interacting with others and establishing friendships are very important activities that add meaning to life. While it is important for Turks to achieve a goal, it is just as important to consider what one receives from the process of achieving it. Growth as a person, and establishing and maintaining good relationships make the goal worth attaining. In this sense, Turks can be viewed as present oriented, valuing what is happening in the present over a possible future occurrence.

D. Direct/Open vs. Indirect/Tactful

Americans pride themselves on dealing with problems as well as personal matters in a direct and open way. Getting a problem out on the table at a business meeting and directly confronting the people involved is seen as an effective way of getting things done and maintaining the relationship. "Clearing the air" is seen as a positive action. They also do not hesitate to disclose information about themselves, even to strangers.

In Turkey, by comparison, being indirect and tactful is preferred. Confrontation is avoided to preserve the harmony in relationships. Being direct is judged as being rude and insulting, giving no value to the relationship and the other person's feelings. The impact of one's actions on the other person is considered as important as getting the job done. When a dispute does erupt, it tends to be bitter. Therefore, a third person is called upon at times to mediate the differences. Because of this value, Americans may feel frustrated at being unable to get direct answers to their questions.

E. Disclosing vs. Face Saving/Honor

Americans generally feel free to state whether or not they know something. There is usually no negative connotation attached to it, on the contrary, one is encouraged to ask questions. For example, "The only stupid question is the one you don't ask," illustrates this point. Although most Americans do not enjoy even "constructive" criticism, this value sanctions criticism of, for example, job performance.

To a Turk, it is more important to save face and honor. One therefore tries at all times to appear competent and knowing. Consequently, one should criticize a Turk only when necessary, and usually not in front of others.

F. Informal vs. Formal

Americans tend to be informal in their relationships. It is not unusual for an American to greet a stranger with a smile and a "Hi!" After the first introductions, people are usually called by their first names. Dress is often quite casual, as is the style of entertaining. In that regard, acting informally with guests is seen as a compliment.

The foregoing comments do not hold true in Turkish culture. Until people know each other well, interactions are kept on a level which would be considered quite formal in the United States. People are addressed formally, and dress is more formal. Because Turkish culture is group-oriented, much of personal interaction is prescribed by traditions of the culture. This aspect is illustrated by the many customary phrases that exist in Turkish which are expected to be used in certain situations, particularly in greeting and parting.

G. Assertive vs. Passive

Americans pride themselves on being assertive. This takes the form of speaking up for oneself, one's beliefs and about one's qualifications.

Turks value being more modest with respect to one's achievements, expecting their friends to put forth their credentials and speak well of them. Sometimes Americans may be seen as impolite in this regard. Consequently, a Turk's résumé may offer only basic factual information. His friends, professors and co-workers are expected to be the real source of information about him. This value complements the indirectness and tactfulness discussed previously.

H. Casual Friendships vs. Deep Friendships

Americans are accustomed to short-term, casual relationships that involve comparatively few reciprocal obligations. In part this may be a reflection of the transient nature of American society and the desire for privacy. It is not unusual to know many people casually, but only a few on a deeper basis. Americans tend to avoid mutual dependency with others, except for close family members. Co-workers constitute an important social group for many Americans.

In Turkey, relationships take longer to form, but they are assumed to be made on a long-term basis. In the initial stages of a relationship, Turks may act in what appears to be a formal manner. However, once they begin to know the other person, they become more deeply involved in the relationship. One assumes certain mutual responsibilities and obligations as a part of the relationship. Dependence is seen as strength and fostered by parents in their children. One's strength comes from one's personal and professional network.

I. Equality vs. Hierarchy

Americans profess that everyone is "created equal" and strive for that ideal to be true. The American Revolution was in part a rejection of a political system based on monarchy. The ideal is that one's status is determined by one's accomplishments, not by one's station of life at birth.

Turks, by comparison, are more comfortable with vertical, hierarchical relationships. They value status and authority over equality. Parents are shown respect and are deferred to at all times. Within the work group, the boss is looked up to for decisions and respected for his/her status. The opinions of older as well as educated people are respected. It is important for a Turk to know the hierarchy of the members of a group, because it determines how he/she will relate to them.

J. Competition vs. Cooperation

Americans believe that competition is good. It motivates people to do their best, knowing that others are striving to do likewise. The American system of free-enterprise is based on this belief, and it permeates the whole culture. A competitive culture lends much to the sense of individualism which was discussed as a value earlier in this section.

In a group oriented culture, such as Turkey, cooperation carries a great deal of importance. This group affiliation, which was discussed earlier, displays itself in the subordination of the individual's goals to those of the group. Although Turks dislike competition within their own groups, it can be intense between different groups. The rivalries between prominent soccer teams illustrate this point.

K. Optimistic vs. Faith/Fatalistic

Americans are optimistic that they can achieve and have anything to which they set their minds, energy and skill. The Puritan idea that anything is possible with hard work is deeply rooted in the American culture. The resulting optimistic, self-starting manner manifests itself in pragmatic behavior. Americans are often more interested in whether something works, rather than in constraints of tradition, history or religion. Americans also strive to dominate nature using science and technology. When nature cannot be dominated, such as in the case of wind or hurricanes, Americans strive to predict it.

Turks, partially because of the teachings of Islam, have faith in a higher power which controls the destiny of man. The common saying, "İnşallah" (God willing), conveys this message. Existing in harmony with nature, rather than trying to change natural phenomena, is commonly accepted. More reliance is placed on traditional explanations of nature's happenings. This value, however, is changing with the rapid industrialization of Turkey.

IV.
CULTURAL EPISODES

How to Use the Cultural Episodes

This section contains 73 cross-cultural episodes involving Americans in Turkey. Each episode depicts a cross-cultural interaction that demonstrates cultural differences. These episodes were designed to prepare Americans to interact with Turks more effectively in a variety of settings. The episodes are divided into five categories which the authors consider to be the most significant areas of cultural adjustment. They are Invitations, In the Workplace, In Public, Traveling, and Adjustment. The authors hope that the reader will find the episodes interesting and often humorous. Presenting the cultural differences in the form of short stories is an enjoyable experience for the reader and should also create a more lasting awareness of the cultural issues presented.

One should read each episode carefully and choose the best answer to the question posed at the end of the episode. The reader then should turn to the next page and read **only** the discussion corresponding to that choice. If this is not given as the best answer, the reader should then review the episode and make another choice. This procedure should be repeated until the best answer is found. Many of the alternate answers also contain valuable information even though they are not the best answers. It is therefore strongly suggested that even if the reader chooses the best answer on the first or the second try, the alternative discussions should also be reviewed.

A. Invitations

1   AN AMERICAN TRADITION

The Smiths invited Jim's co-worker Ali and his wife for dinner. Jim liked Ali in part because he was somewhat conservative, like him. Jim and his wife decided to treat their Turkish guests to a traditional American meal of ham, potatoes, green beans, and apple pie with California wine from the American base.

Ali and his wife arrived at 6 PM for dinner. As the evening progressed, they were able to overcome the initial uneasiness of first social encounters. Although everything was going well, the Smiths noticed that Ali and his wife did not touch much of the food or even sample the wine. The Smiths felt unappreciated and puzzled.

Why did Ali and his wife decline the food and drink?

1. They were being polite by having little to eat or drink with new acquaintances.

2. Islam prohibits the consumption of pork and alcohol.

3. They were not accustomed to American food and wine and were afraid to try them.

4. It was too early for the Turkish guests to have dinner, and they were not yet hungry.

1   AN AMERICAN TRADITION

1. This could be the case, since it is not polite to take additional servings of food or drink unless insisted upon by the hostess. We do not know, however, if Mrs. Smith knew to offer more food and drink. There is a better answer. Please choose again.

2. Islam prohibits the consumption of pork and alcohol, and most Turks are Moslems. Since Turkey is a secular state, however, people can choose whether or not to strictly obey the rules of Islam. Most Turks do not eat pork, but alcohol use is quite prevalent. In this case, since Ali and his wife are quite conservative, chances are they do not use alcohol. This is the best answer.

3. This could be possibly correct, since some people are not very adventurous in trying new things. However, Ali and his wife would probably at least sample the food, to avoid offending their hosts. There is a more relevant point. Please choose again.

4. This could be correct since Turks do eat dinner later, at about 8 PM. However, this would not fully explain why the Turks failed to even politely sample the food. There is a more likely answer. Please choose again.

2   WHISPERS IN THE KITCHEN

Carl Johnson had been working as a project engineer in İstanbul
for two months. The first several weeks were very difficult for Carl
and his wife Alice. They felt very lonely and isolated.

Recently Carl and Ali, the Turkish assistant plant manager, had
become good friends. One morning while discussing the replace-
ment of some pumps, Ali said, "By the way Carl, my wife and I
would like to invite you for dinner next Saturday." Carl said that
it was probably all right, and he was going to check with his wife
that night.

Carl and Alice ate lunch at a seafood restaurant on the Bosphorus and then went to a movie matinée. Because Ali had not
mentioned a time, Carl and Alice arrived at Ali's home after the
movie at 6 PM. When they knocked on the door, Ali and his
wife Selma greeted them warmly, but looked somewhat surprised.
After serving Jim and Alice drinks, Ali and Selma disappeared
into the kitchen. Carl and Alice heard some whispers and did not
know what was going on.

What would explain Ali and Selma's behavior?

1. Ali and Selma were not expecting Carl and his wife, because
   Carl had not given Ali a final acceptance of the invitation.

2. Carl and Alice arrived too early for dinner.

3. Ali and Selma were surprised that Carl and Alice did not bring
   a present.

4. Ali and Selma were amazed by the casual dress of Carl and
   Alice.

2   WHISPERS IN THE KITCHEN

1. This is possible but not very plausible, because Ali would have made sure that they were not coming before assuming it. Please choose again.

2. Carl and Alice probably assumed dinner time to be the same in Turkey as in the United States, which is not the case. Many of our assumptions are unconscious, and we do not recognize them as a cultural issue until we are faced with another culture. Turks generally eat dinner at about 8 PM, and they probably assumed Carl and Alice did likewise. This is the best answer.

3. This is probably not the case, since a present is not required. It is nice to bring some flowers or candy, but guests are not obligated to do so. In any event, the Turks would not feel that way. Please choose again.

4. It is not stated what Carl and Alice wore, but the episode suggests that they came directly from the movie. When visiting, especially for the first time, dress is expected to be somewhat formal. Women usually wear nice dresses, and men wear dress pants and a nice shirt, if not a suit. There is a better answer. Please choose again.

3   THE BURSA TEA PARTY

Mary decided to have a tea party for her Turkish friends in Bursa. She had been to their homes and felt very welcome ever since she and her husband Jerry had arrived in Turkey five months earlier. Mary had prepared herself for life in Bursa before leaving the United States, realizing that cultural knowledge would help her tremendously. This knowledge had served her well in feeling accepted by the women in Bursa. As she invited the women, most of them had answered, "İnşallah" (God Willing) and smiled, which she had taken to mean "yes."

The day of the party finally arrived, and she was looking forward to it with great anticipation. An hour after the party started, however, about a quarter of the guests had not shown up. She felt hurt as well as angry at their lack of consideration.

Why did the women not attend her party?

1. Something came up, but they did not consider it necessary to notify the hostess.

2. "İnşallah" can mean not only "yes" but also a tactful "maybe."

3. Their husbands did not permit them to attend.

4. The women were running late.

3   THE BURSA TEA PARTY

1. This is a good answer. The women might have considered it unimportant to notify Mary. There is, however, a more plausible answer which explains why they would not notify the hostess. Please choose again.

2. Because of the concern for keeping good relationships and not hurting anyone's feelings, "İnşallah" is used quite frequently by many Turks. This word covers both definite "yes" and uncertain "maybe" situations. The Turkish women would possibly use this term to be polite and indirect in giving a "no" answer. This is the best answer.

3. This is probably not the case. Please choose again.

4. This could be true since time is not adhered to as strictly as in the United States. Americans have a hard time being as time flexible as Turks are. In this context, however, an hour delay would also be considered excessive by Turkish standards. There is a better answer. Please choose again.

4   THE WEDDING

Tom and Janet spent hours one day shopping for an exquisite
wedding gift for Tom's Turkish counterpart Veli. After purchasing an expensive marble vase, Tom said to his wife, "It is well
worth the effort and expense. Veli is my best friend here." He
also thought that it would be prestigious when the presents were
opened in front of the guests.

After a short wedding ceremony the guests were invited to the
reception which took place in a big hall. After the opening dance,
the bride and groom started walking from table to table, shaking
hands with the guests. The guests presented their gifts when it
was their turn to greet the bride and groom. Tom and Janet
noticed that none of the presents were opened or displayed other
than the jewelry and the Turkish currency which were attached
to the bride's dress. The bride took the present from Tom and
Janet and gave it to her sister who collected the presents and put
them away.

Tom and Janet thought it was a Turkish custom to open the
presents, since the gift that they had taken to the Turkish plant
manager's house the week before was opened in front of them.

Can you clarify this Turkish custom for Tom and Janet?

1. Although the gifts would be opened at any other public gathering, wedding gifts are opened in the presence of the wedding
   couple and close family.

2. The opening of the wedding gifts does not take place until late
   at night, as the party comes to an end.

3. If gifts are brought by more than one person, they are not
   publicly opened.

4. It is considered bad luck to open wedding gifts in public.

4   THE WEDDING

1. Weddings are not an exception to the rules of gift opening. Please choose again.

2. This is not the custom. Please choose again.

3. In order not to hurt anyone's feelings by opening the presents publicly and inviting comparison of the gifts, they are not opened. This is not true if there is only one gift; in this latter case, it is usually opened in front of the guests. This is the best answer.

4. There is no such belief. Please choose again.

5   A DOZEN ROSES

Ron, Kim, and their two children, five year old Mary and two year old Michael, were living in İzmir. Ron was assigned to the NATO contingent based there. One evening they were invited to the home of Ahmet, Ron's colleague. Looking forward to a pleasant evening, Kim arranged for an American teenager to babysit Mary and Michael.

Kim and Ron arrived at Ahmet's house with a beautifully wrapped bouquet of a dozen roses. Ahmet and his wife Selma greeted them warmly at the door. Selma asked about their children. Kim explained that a teenager was babysitting them. Selma graciously accepted the flowers, but Ron and Kim sensed a slight puzzlement on the part of Ahmet and Selma.

Why did Ahmet and Selma seem puzzled?

1. Selma was surprised because the American couple brought an even number of flowers.

2. Ahmet and Selma were unfamiliar with the concept of "babysitting."

3. Ahmet and Selma were slightly offended by the absence of Mary and Michael.

4. A bouquet of flowers is appropriate only for wedding celebrations.

5. The Turks were surprised that Ron was not wearing his military uniform.

5   A DOZEN ROSES

1. Although some people may consider it important, bringing an odd number of flowers is not a widely held custom in Turkey. There is a better answer. Please choose again.

2. The "babysitter" concept does not exist in Turkey. The grand-parents or other family members may watch the child, but they are not compensated for this. There is, however, a better choice. Please choose again.

3. Children are highly valued and are assumed to be included in this type of invitation. Ahmet and Selma would look forward to seeing the whole family. This is the best choice.

4. Flowers are appropriate for almost any occasion. Please choose again.

5. This is not very likely. Please choose again.

6   THE FERRYBOAT RIDE

It was 2 PM on a lovely Saturday afternoon in İstanbul. Keith, Sally and their three children were preparing for a trip to the Bosphorus to take a ferryboat ride. Just as they were about to leave, there was a knock on the door. It was Keith's friend from work, İbrahim, his wife Nezihe and their two children. İbrahim said that they were visiting relatives in the area and wanted to stop in. Keith felt very close to İbrahim, and the two families had visited each other for dinner many times. Keith did not want to offend İbrahim, although he felt it was rude for them to just drop in. They invited the family in, and Sally served them something to drink. Keith complimented İbrahim and Nezihe on how their children were so polite and well behaved. İbrahim and Nezihe were apparently enjoying themselves, as were Keith and Sally. As evening approached, however, Sally could not help but feel resentful that their ferryboat ride on this lovely afternoon was not going to happen.

Why did İbrahim's family drop in unexpectedly?

1. In Turkey, it is acceptable to make unannounced visits on weekends.

2. In Turkey, close friends may drop in unexpectedly.

3. Since İbrahim and Keith were close friends, İbrahim thought that Keith would inform him of any conflicts.

4. İbrahim and Nezihe were inconsiderate.

6   THE FERRYBOAT RIDE

1. This answer is partially correct. The best answer explains why this is so. Please choose again.

2. Relationships are very important in Turkey, and this custom is one example of that. In general, close friends are free to drop in without invitation. Friendships may take longer to develop, but once formed they are long lasting and have strong commitments of loyalty and service behind them. This is the best answer.

3. This is more a reflection of American culture than Turkish. Americans feel free to directly state that they have other plans, whereas Turks would not make friends feel unwelcome because of other plans. Please choose again.

4. This is not correct. As a matter of fact they were indicating, by their actions, that they consider Keith and his family as close friends. Otherwise they would not pay them the compliment of dropping in unannounced. Please choose again.

7   LİMON KOLONYASI

James and Patty had lived in Belgium for three years before James was assigned to a new project in Konya. They were eager to settle in and make Turkish friends.

They were very excited when a co-worker of James, Cemal, invited them to dinner at his home; this was their first invitation in Turkey. It was a rainy day, and they made their way from the car across the muddy sidewalk to Cemal's front door. Cemal and his wife Nezihe were newlyweds. They greeted their guests warmly. James and Patty were most anxious to make a good impression. As Nezihe was taking their coats, they passed a row of slippers by the door. After they were seated, Nezihe went to the buffet and returned with a bottle of Limon Kolonyası (a lemon-scented light cologne with a high alcohol content that is applied to the hands and face as a refresher) and offered it first to Patty and then to James. Cemal and Nezihe were very hospitable all evening, and James and Patty really enjoyed themselves.

What were the slippers doing at the door?

1. The slippers were for use in visiting the bathroom.

2. Nezihe was rushed and forgot to put them away.

3. The slippers were for use on wet and muddy days.

4. The slippers were for the guests.

5. The slippers were for the use of Moslem guests while praying.

7   LİMON KOLONYASI

1. Although there may be special slippers for use in the bathroom, they would always be kept inside the bathroom and not by the main entrance. Please choose again.

2. Americans would tend to make sure slippers are out of sight when entertaining, but Turks do not. Please choose again to find out why.

3. This is only partially correct, and the best answer provides the explanation. Please choose again.

4. Since cleanliness is very important in Turkish homes, shoes worn in the street are usually not worn in the house. Slippers are kept at the door for family members as well as for guests. People entering the house are expected to take off their shoes and put on slippers. Cemal and Nezihe were being polite hosts in not saying anything. Guests are highly honored, and everything possible is done to make them feel welcome. This is the best answer.

5. In this case, the slippers have nothing to do with prayer. Please choose again.

8   A CHARMING PERSON

Pam and Chuck, a young American couple, had both been working
for the same company in Turkey for the past three months. One
of the Turkish mechanics in Chuck's division, Mahmut, invited
them for dinner. When Chuck and Pamela arrived at Mahmut's
house, he was drinking beer on the balcony and his wife Ayşe
was working in the kitchen. Later they noticed Ayşe setting the
dinner table and watching over the meal. Mahmut made no effort
to help his wife. This started to bother Pam. During the entire
dinner Ayşe did all the serving. After dinner they started talking
about various issues. Learning that Ayşe was a teacher at the
school their daughter was attending, Pam and Chuck asked her
some questions about the school. Ayşe was a charming person
and well versed in a variety of topics. The conversation started
excluding Mahmut, and he became increasingly quiet. After a
while, Ayşe, too, became quiet and reserved.

How would you explain Ayşe's behavior?

1. Ayşe became quiet when she realized that she had been bragging.

2. Ayşe was enjoying the attention given her by Pam and Chuck,
   and realized that her husband was feeling ignored.

3. Ayşe felt sad when she sensed that she had more in common
   with Pam and Chuck than with her own husband.

4. Ayşe realized that she had deviated from expected cultural
   norms.

8   A CHARMING PERSON

1. There is nothing to indicate that Ayşe had been bragging. Please choose again.

2. This could be true, since most people enjoy having attention paid to them. There is a more important point, however, please choose again.

3. There is nothing stated about Ayşe feeling sad. Moreover, it would seem unlikely that three people from two different cultures in a first time meeting would have more in common than a husband and wife. Please choose again.

4. This is the most likely reason for Ayşe's behavior because Turkey tends to be a male dominated society. Ayşe had behaved like a submissive Turkish wife until the conversation turned to her profession. Her husband's withdrawal from the conversation signaled Ayşe that she had overstepped her role.

9   I AM NOT HUNGRY

One day Ali invited his American colleague Steve and his wife
Linda to his house for dinner. While they were eating, someone
knocked at the door. When Ali's wife Emine opened the door,
they saw Ali's brother Mehmet standing there. Mehmet had just
arrived from another town. Ali introduced his brother to the
guests.

Emine asked Mehmet to join them for dinner, but Mehmet refused, saying, "I am not hungry." For a while Steve and Linda
watched Emine insisting and Mehmet refusing to eat. Finally,
Mehmet agreed to join them, but warned Emine not to put too
much food on his plate. Steve and Linda became very confused
when Mehmet ate fairly large portions of everything.

Can you explain Mehmet's behavior?

1. Mehmet was ashamed that he had dropped in unannounced
   when Ali had guests, and therefore he tried not to be a bother.

2. Mehmet felt neglected because Steve and Linda were the guests
   of honor.

3. Mehmet was reluctant to eat in the presence of strangers.

4. Mehmet was behaving as a proper guest.

5. Although Mehmet was not hungry, he ate because he did not
   want to hurt Emine's feelings.

9   I AM NOT HUNGRY

1. It is very acceptable for family members to drop in unannounced, even when guests are present, so this would not explain his behavior. An inadequate supply of food was probably not a concern of his either, since there is usually more food cooked than could be possibly eaten. Offering generous amounts of food is an important part of showing hospitality. Please choose again.

2. There is no established guest of honor concept in Turkish culture. In general, every guest is considered important, and no individual is singled out for special recognition. Please choose again.

3. This is probably not the case since Turks are generally warm and hospitable people. Please choose again.

4. It is usually assumed that one comes to a house to visit and enjoy the company of others, and not only to eat. A proper guest does not accept food until it has been offered several times, just as Mehmet did. The ritual of offering food and the guest's initial refusals, are all a part of the expected behavior for a hostess and guest. This is the best answer.

5. This may be true, because it would be rude of a guest not to at least taste what the hostess has cooked. Turkish women pride themselves on their cooking skills and derive great pleasure watching people appreciate the result of their efforts. However, it is stated that the portions were large, so there is a better answer than polite eating. Please select another answer.

10   A CHILL IN THE AIR

Suzanne and Phil were invited to dinner at the home of Phil's
Turkish co-worker Selim. Phil and Selim started drinking Efes
beer. After several beers they started to casually discuss politics at the plant. The topic of their conversation soon forged
into Turkish economic development. Selim expressed his frustra-
tions at what he perceived to be a cumbersome bureaucracy. Phil
agreed with Selim and added, "The government seems to have a
big finger in every pot." Phil was really happy to talk with a Turk
who shared his viewpoints.

Meanwhile Suzanne followed Ayşe into the kitchen from the patio
where they had been talking about Turkish food. Ayşe started
feeling uncomfortable having Suzanne in the kitchen. Suzanne
sensed her discomfort and started helping Ayşe in order to ease
the tension. They continued their conversation about Turkish
food. Suzanne said, "We buy canned food from Europe, because
we feel that the quality is much better." When the couples sat
down for dinner, Phil and Suzanne felt a chill in the air.

Why was there a chill in the air?

1. Ayşe felt that Suzanne invaded her privacy by following her
   into the kitchen.

2. Ayşe was hurt by Suzanne's comments about the quality of
   Turkish food.

3. Selim did not appreciate Phil's comments about Turkey .

4. Although Turks may criticize certain aspects of their own culture, comments by foreigners are not appreciated.

10   A CHILL IN THE AIR

1. A guest in a Turkish home is to be waited on, and the kitchen is considered to be the private domain of the hostess. Entertaining in Turkey follows more formal rules than in the United States. This is a good answer. There is, however, a better one. Please choose again.

2. This is a good answer. It is insensitive of Suzanne to suggest that the quality of food is not good in Turkey. Turkey produces a wonderful variety of foodstuffs. For a better answer, however, please choose again.

3. Phil was discourteous in openly criticizing Selim's country. This is a good answer. There is a more comprehensive answer, though. Please choose again.

4. As a foreigner, it is best to only listen when Turks express views on their own country. Strong nationalistic pride is an important Turkish value. This is the best answer.

11   THE UNEXPECTED GIFT

Chuck and Jill had lived in Eskişehir for six months. One evening they were invited to dinner at the home of Chuck's boss Ahmet. Ahmet and his wife Nesrin greeted them warmly. Jill presented Nesrin with an expensive Austrian crystal candy dish that she had bought during their last vacation in Europe. Jill had never met Ahmet and Nesrin, and felt uncomfortable about what to say. After the small talk seemed to die down, Jill, in desperation, commented on how beautiful a flower vase looked on the table, even though she did not like it. Nesrin thanked her and said that it was a wedding gift and meant a lot to them.

A month later, Chuck and Jill returned the dinner invitation. As Ahmet and Nesrin arrived, Nesrin presented Jill with a beautifully wrapped package. Thinking that it was the Turkish custom not to open presents until the guests leave, Jill opened it after the Turks left and was dismayed to find it to be a vase similar to the one she had "admired" in their home. She knew it was expensive. She felt helpless knowing that she could do nothing but keep it.

How could Jill have avoided this situation?

1. Jill should have opened the gift in front of the guests.

2. She should have been more selective about the object of her praise.

3. Jill should have dealt with her uneasiness by being silent.

4. Jill could have avoided it by not taking a lavish gift and thus making Nesrin feel obligated to do likewise.

11   THE UNEXPECTED GIFT

1. This would not solve the problem. If Jill opened the gift in the presence of the guests she would still be faced with receiving an unwanted gift since it would be impolite to refuse it. Please choose again.

2. The food being served that evening would have been a good choice for praise. Being aware that the object of praise may become a gift, makes it important to carefully select what one admires. There is a better choice, however, please choose again.

3. Nesrin and Ahmet brought a similar vase as a present because Nesrin thought that Jill really liked the vase she saw in their home. There are many uneasy situations in a new culture, and hasty attempts to deal with them may create more problems. This is the best answer.

4. An expensive gift is usually not appropriate for a dinner invitation. It may leave the other person feeling obligated to reciprocate. A box of candy or flowers is usually more appropriate. This is probably not the reason, however, why the vase was given. Please choose again for a better answer.

12   POTLUCK

Alice was an outgoing person and had made quite a few friends since arriving in Ankara. She decided to host a potluck to get her American and Turkish friends together for lunch. Alice wanted to include the wives of the two Turkish plant managers who worked with her husband, since they had invited her for tea when she first arrived. She also wanted to include three of her Turkish neighbors. Alice called everyone and invited them to the potluck. Her American friends thought it was a great idea. The Turkish women replied, "İnşallah" (God Willing). The lunch time came and went with only the American women showing up.

What was the most probable reason that the Turkish women did not attend?

1. The Turkish women were from different social classes and did not want to mix.

2. İnşallah is an ambiguous response which can mean either "yes" or "maybe."

3. Expecting a guest to bring food is considered impolite in Turkey.

4. The Turkish women did not understand the concept of potluck and therefore decided not to attend.

5. The Turkish women felt uncomfortable about socializing with a group of Americans.

12   POTLUCK

1. This may be true, because the hierarchical structure is carefully observed. However, the Turkish women did not know who else would be in attendance, so just on that basis, there is a more plausible answer. Please choose again.

2. This is correct, and perhaps it was used to conceal the real reason they were not going to attend. However, that would not explain why none of the Turkish women showed up. Please choose again.

3. The potluck concept does not exist in Turkey. A guest is a very important person and is not expected to bring food when invited. The most probable reason the Turkish women did not show up is that they were offended. This is the best answer.

4. They may not have understood the concept of potluck, but then Alice probably would ask them to bring something, which would give them an idea of what a potluck is. Please choose again for a better reason.

5. This is an unlikely reason, since Turkish women are very sociable. Moreover, in this particular situation the wives of the plant managers had already hosted her for tea when she first arrived. Please choose again.

13   COFFEE AND BROWNIES

Ann was invited to the house of her Turkish neighbor Sacide for afternoon tea. Sacide had set a beautiful table with flowers and lovely cakes and cookies and delicious Turkish tea in little glasses. Sacide kept offering food and drink to her even after Ann had said that she had had enough. Ann wondered how Sacide kept her slim figure.

Ann was looking forward to returning Sacide's hospitality by entertaining her with some American coffee and brownies. She went out of her way to buy some slippers for Sacide, similar to those Sacide had offered her. Ann dressed for the afternoon in a comfortable pair of jeans and a sweatshirt.

Sacide arrived wearing a blue dress and carrying a small bouquet of flowers. Ann offered her some coffee. Sacide smiled sweetly but declined. Ann was puzzled. She then offered her some brownies, explaining that they were a favorite dessert in America. Again, Sacide declined. They chatted for a bit, but later Sacide grew increasingly quiet as if something were wrong. Ann had nothing to say, so she was relieved when Sacide said she had to leave to start dinner.

Why did Sacide decline the coffee and brownies?

1. Ann's casual dress made Sacide feel that she was not an appreciated guest.

2. Sacide wanted to keep her trim figure.

3. Sacide was hesitant to try American coffee and brownies because they were new to her.

4. Sacide was being polite and was waiting for Ann to repeat her offer of food and drink.

5. It was the month of fasting and Sacide could not eat.

13   COFFEE AND BROWNIES

1. Sacide may have felt this way because of Ann's casual dress. As covered earlier, Turks dress more formally in public than Americans, but this would not keep her from accepting the food and drink and acting as a polite guest. Please choose again.

2. In Turkish culture the slenderness American women strive for might be considered unhealthy (however, this value may be changing in recent years). Besides Sacide would not act as an impolite guest and fail to even sample the food. There is a better answer. Please choose again.

3. It would be impolite for a Turkish guest not to try at least a small amount of food and drink offered by the hostess. This, therefore, is not a correct answer. Please choose again.

4. In general, it would be improper to accept the food after only the first offer. A guest would accept food and drink after it has been offered several times. This is the culturally appropriate behavior and the best answer.

5. There is nothing in the incident to indicate that it is Ramazan, the month of fasting. Sacide would have told Ann if she were fasting and would have declined the invitation. Please choose again.

14   AN ILLNESS IN THE FAMILY

Julie and her husband Mike invited their Turkish friends Osman
and Selma Fırat for dinner. The Fırats arrived 50 minutes late.
Julie and Mike were not very happy with this. The dinner was
cold, and Julie had to warm it up again. The Fırats entered the
house and looked at the floor, as if they were trying to find something. They then started taking off their shoes. Mike told them,
"We do not take our shoes off in the house." Selma apologized
for their late arrival, explaining that Osman's mother, who lived
with them, was ill. Osman's father also lived with them, and they
had been waiting for him to come home. Osman noted that both
of his parents were elderly and frail, with frequent bouts of illness.
Mike said that his mother had been in a nursing home for several
years due to poor health. Osman stated that he felt it was his
duty to take care of his parents.

When they sat down to eat, Mike started eating immediately,
since Julie had fixed his favorite meal. Dinner passed pleasantly,
but the Fırats left shortly thereafter.

Why did the Fırats leave early?

1. **Osman and Selma realized that Julie and Mike were upset with
   their late arrival.**

2. **The Fırats were uncomfortable with the "nursing home" concept.**

3. **The Fırats were worried about Osman's mother.**

4. **The Fırats felt that they were not sincerely welcomed since
   they were not offered slippers, and Mike started eating first.**

14   AN ILLNESS IN THE FAMILY

1. This may be true but they would not necessarily leave early because of it. Please choose again.

2. This is a possible answer, since "nursing homes" carry a negative connotation in Turkey. People are expected to take care of their family members and are thought of very poorly if they do not meet this responsibility. Nursing homes are often only for people who have no one to care for them. There is a more likely reason for their early departure, though. Please choose again.

3. Relationships are very important in Turkish culture, and the Fırats would want to be with their ill mother. Responsibility to others comes before individual considerations. This concern would, however, conflict with their feeling that a polite guest does not leave immediately after eating. The Fırats would feel obligated to stay awhile, as they did, but might consider it appropriate to then leave because the illness was unexpected. This is the most plausible explanation.

4. It is customary to offer slippers to guests when they enter the house, as well as waiting for the guests to eat first. However, since the Fırats are already friends, and would be trying to act as polite guests, it is unlikely that it would cause them to leave early. Please choose again.

15   AFİYET OLSUN

Kabul Günü is an afternoon tea party which is hosted by different neighborhood women on various days of the month according to an agreed upon schedule. It was Katie's landlady, Yıldız Hanım's (Hanım is a title used for women after the first name and corresponds to Miss, Mrs., or Ms. in English) turn to host the party. Katie wanted to embarrass neither herself nor her landlady at the party, and therefore asked her for a quick orientation to appropriate behavior. Although she was still somewhat apprehensive, Katie decided to plunge in.

Katie arrived with the brownies that she had made and was introduced to a roomful of neighborhood ladies who were all staring at her. When she started serving the tea, she noticed that the stares continued. As she offered the tea, she said, "Buyrun" (help yourself). The ladies seemed pleased. Later, when she collected the empty glasses, the ladies commented on how good the tea and brownies were. She responded with "Afiyet Olsun" (good appetite). The afternoon went well. The Turkish ladies were very interested in Katie and asked her a number of personal questions concerning her job, salary, and marital status. Although she felt a little uncomfortable with the questions, she answered most of them anyway. Several of the women indicated that Katie was welcome to their tea parties as well.

Why was Katie accepted by the Turkish women?

1. She made every attempt to use her limited Turkish.

2. She answered their personal questions.

3. Katie did not let their stares bother her.

4. Katie behaved in accordance with Turkish cultural expectations.

15   AFİYET OLSUN

1. Turks are very pleased when Americans show that they are
   attempting to speak Turkish. Any attempt, no matter how
   slight, is met with appreciation. There is a better answer,
   however, please choose again.

2. Katie, by answering their personal questions, was recognizing
   that although such questions are considered impolite in the
   United States, they may simply indicate curiosity in Turkey. It
   is, however, acceptable to nicely indicate that you do not care
   to answer certain questions. This is a good choice, but there
   is a better one. Please choose again.

3. Staring, while considered rude in the United States, indicates
   curiosity in Turkey. By not letting herself be bothered by the
   stares, she allowed the ladies to become comfortable with her.
   This is a good choice, but there is a better one. Please choose
   again.

4. This choice includes all the other choices and is therefore the
   best one. Katie is an example of how adhering to cultural
   expectations allows one to be accepted and therefore given a
   chance to take part in the culture. It is not possible to adhere
   to these expectations in every situation, but carefully deciding
   which situations will provide the opportunities one is seeking
   may pay great dividends in the long run.

16   A LAVISH PARTY

A group of young Turkish engineers was sent to the United States
to be trained in the specifics of the technology that would be used
in the new joint venture. The American instructors were very
excited and decided to throw a lavish welcoming dinner. They
hired a caterer specializing in Middle Eastern cuisine. To make
their guests feel at home, they decided to serve the meal in a
Middle Eastern atmosphere. The day before the party, the caterer
instructed them on how to eat the meal properly with their hands.

When the Turks arrived at the dinner, they were surprised to see
the arrangements. As the party progressed, the conversation became increasingly relaxed. Tom, a young engineer, asked Hacer,
a Turkish engineer, how it felt to be out of her veil since she was
wearing a stylish western dress. She smiled but was distracted by
the waiter offering her more refreshments. Tom then turned to
the other Turks and joined their conversation. At one point, attempting to be polite, Tom indicated that he would learn Turkish
if it were not for the Arabic script. The party continued, but it
was apparent that the Turks were becoming more distant. After
the party the Americans felt very discouraged and wondered what
went wrong.

What went wrong at the party?

1. The Turks were offended at the implication that all Turkish
   women are veiled.

2. The Turks were surprised at being served an Arab style meal.

3. The Turks were unhappy with the Americans' ignorance about
   Turkey.

4. Being confused with Arabs offended the Turks.

16   A LAVISH PARTY

1. This shows lack of knowledge of Turkey, and a stereotype of the Middle Eastern woman, and may be offensive. There is a better answer, though. Please choose again.

2. Turkish culture is different from Arab culture which dominates most of the Middle East. The meal indicates a lack of awareness on the part of the Americans. For example, in Turkey people usually do not eat with their hands. This meal, therefore, would not create a good first impression. Please choose again, however, for a better answer.

3. This is a good choice. The Americans were indicating their lack of knowledge of Turkey, even though they had tried hard to welcome the Turks. Learning something about Turkey beforehand would have pleased the Turks more than the lavish dinner. Please choose again for a better answer.

4. The Turkish Republic was formed in 1923, with Atatürk as the leader. At that time Turkey turned its face to the West. In general, Turks want to be thought of as European more than Middle Eastern. Along with many other changes, Atatürk's reforms outlawed the wearing of the fez for men, and the veil for women. The Turkish alphabet is similar to that used in English. Eating, in general, is done Western style, not on the floor or with hands. Of course, Turkey is a diverse land, and one could find, in the smaller villages of eastern Turkey, a more Middle Eastern approach to life. This is the best choice.

B. In the Workplace

We hope that you are enjoying this book.
Please continue!

17   THE FIRST IMPRESSION

Jim had just arrived in İstanbul on a work assignment. Although
he knew his job well and had received his degrees from respected
universities in his field, he felt a little insecure about the prospect
of dealing with Turks. He was introduced to Kadir, his counterpart, and wanted to make sure they got off on the right foot.
He told Kadir that he had a B.S. degree from the University of
Illinois and a M.S. degree from Cal Tech. He explained that he
had been with his company for ten years and had been a successful supervisor for the last three. He then asked Kadir about his
background. Kadir said it was not really important and changed
the subject. Jim sensed that their first meeting had not been a
success, although he had no idea why.

Why did Kadir act in this manner?

1. Kadir did not think that his credentials were as good as Jim's
   and was reluctant to talk about them.

2. Kadir was displaying Turkish modesty.

3. Kadir considered the topic to be inappropriate for the first
   meeting.

4. Kadir was offended by Jim's bragging.

17   THE FIRST IMPRESSION

1. Although this may seem to be a reasonable conclusion from the American point of view, it is not from the Turkish perspective. Please choose again.

2. There is a difference in what is considered modest behavior in Turkey as compared with the United States. Modesty is highly valued in Turkey and includes not speaking of one's own accomplishments. To do so is considered bragging and inappropriate. Kadir expected that Jim would find out about his qualifications from written information, or by word of mouth from Kadir's friends. Kadir's resume, therefore, would also tend to understate his accomplishments. This is the best answer.

3. This is somewhat true, since in Turkey it is important to establish a personal relationship before dealing with business matters. Please choose again for a better answer.

4. This is the next best answer. Although Jim was acting in an acceptable manner for the United States, his behavior was probably not appropriate by Turkish standards. Being direct and open in stating one's accomplishments is not considered appropriate in Turkish culture. Although Kadir probably did not like Jim's behavior, there is a more direct reason for Kadir's evasive response concerning his own qualifications. Please select another answer.

18   İKİ-BUÇUK ($2\frac{1}{2}$) LİRA

Jim and two other Americans were in Turkey to negotiate a contract for their company. They had been to Turkey on several visits
during the negotiation process and had grown to like Turkey and
the Turks with whom they were dealing. One day, they were
talking with the Turks at the office about the rare coins that
Jim collected as a hobby. One of the Turks, Niyazi, pulled out
a $2\frac{1}{2}$ TL (Turkish Lira) coin to show to Jim, explaining that it
was no longer used because of the high inflation rate. The coin
had Atatürk's famous Independence War picture on one side. Jim
admired the coin and remarked that it was very unique and interesting. Niyazi told him that he could keep it. Jim refused and
tried to return it, but Niyazi insisted that he keep it. Jim felt bad
about having admired it and helpless, since he felt his only choice
was to keep it. He could not understand why Niyazi had given it
to him.

Can you help James understand why he was given the coin?

1. Niyazi knew that Jim was a coin collector.

2. Niyazi gave the coin to Jim as a goodwill gesture to aid the
   contract negotiations.

3. Niyazi was proud of the Independence War scene on the coin
   and wanted to share it with Jim who obviously loved Turkey.

4. Since Jim admired the coin Niyazi gave it to him as a gift.

18   İKİ BUÇUK $(2\frac{1}{2})$ LİRA

1. The incident states that Jim collects coins as a hobby, but this does not explain why Niyazi gave (rather than sold, etc.) the coin to him. This is a possible reason, but please choose again for a better one.

2. This is a plausible answer. There is, however, a better cultural explanation. Please choose again.

3. This is a good choice. Turks are very nationalistic, proud of their history and very happy when Americans indicate a love for their country. For a slightly better answer, however, please choose again.

4. This is the best answer because it can be generalized to almost any situation. If something is admired, there is the possibility that it will be offered as a gift. In this situation, since Jim had no other choice but to look at and admire the coin, he can recognize that it is perfectly fine to enjoy the token of friendship the coin represents. However, in giving and receiving gifts, the employees of a United States company conducting business in a foreign country should consult their company's established policy, including compliance with the Foreign Corrupt Practices Act. See the bibliography (Baruch, 1987; Fadiman, 1986; Perkins, 1987) for additional information.

19   EAST MEETS WEST

Jim was new to Ankara, having just arrived from Wyoming to work on a coal project. He did not know how he felt about being in Turkey, but knew that he loved Wyoming. His hat, boots, and blue jeans, as well as his "rough" language, were all a part of him. There was nothing he loved better than to laugh and joke with his buddies. Everyone loved Bill's sense of humor and true Western flair.

In Ankara, he was determined to be himself and get friendly real quick with the Turks. He slapped them on the back and told some off color jokes and wore his boots, jeans, and hat. When in public Jim always stood out from the rest of the crowd due to his loud manner. It did not take him long to notice people beginning to pull away from him. He was dismayed, because he was accustomed to being the center of attention. He started having second thoughts about being in Ankara.

Why were people pulling away from Jim?

1. Jim's Western style dress was unacceptable attire on the job.

2. Swearing, particularly using God's name, and loud talk are unacceptable to most Turks.

3. Back-slapping occurs only among friends, not new acquaintances.

4. In Turkey, friendships are developed over time and cannot be rushed.

19   EAST MEETS WEST

1. In general, Turks dress more formally than Americans, and Jim would stand out with his Western clothing. There is, however, a more plausible reason. Please choose again.

2. His manner brought him approval in the United States, but the same actions are probably bringing disapproval in Turkey. Cultural awareness is important, and a willingness to refrain from offensive behavior may be necessary for acceptance. Sometimes this might require that the American "cramp his style" from what would be acceptable in the United States. Swearing is usually offensive. Swearing that uses God's name can only be taken as negative. For example, expressions such as "God damn good job" would be understood to mean a bad job. In public, people usually talk quietly, and loud talk is often considered rude. This is the best answer.

3. This is true and may cause people to avoid him. In Turkey relationships are usually formal at the beginning, and new acquaintances do not relate to one another in such a familiar manner. Please choose again.

4. In general, Americans act friendly, smile to passersby, and make friends quickly and easily. This is not the case in Turkey. Friendships must stand the test of time and consequently are formed more slowly than in the United States. There is a better answer, however, please choose again.

20   GET ON WITH IT!

Bill felt very frustrated with his job in Ankara. In the United States, he had been effective in getting the job done well and quickly. Now, however, he noticed that his Turkish counterparts offered him tea, asked about his family and interspersed personal comments during business discussions. The resulting delays led to missed deadlines, and the home office started questioning Bill's managerial skills. When he tried to curtail the diversions, the Turks acted cool and were harder to relate to.

Can you help Bill understand what was going on?

1. The Turkish workers were not as work driven as their American counterparts.

2. The Turkish workers resented having an American boss, especially a pushy one.

3. The Turks were trying first to establish a personal relationship with Bill.

4. The Turks wanted to learn about American life and felt rejected by Bill's behavior.

20   GET ON WITH IT!

1. Turks can be very hard workers, just as Americans, but they have a different value structure in the workplace. To understand what it is, please choose again.

2. It could be true that the workers dislike the boss because he is an American. Americans, however, are generally liked, and the problems are probably more attributable to Bill's personal management style. Please select another response.

3. In order to work with someone effectively, Turks first need a personal relationship. Taking the time to establish this relationship seems like a waste of valuable time to many Americans, but in the long run more will be accomplished. If the boss is perceived as pushy and not interested in developing a relationship, the workers will tend to frustrate his/her demands for action. Recognizing the importance of relationships, and accepting this as a value may help Bill be more effective. This is the best answer.

4. Turks are curious about life in the United States, but there is a better reason. Please choose again.

21   I'LL BE HOME FOR CHRISTMAS

Jerry was sent to Turkey by his company on a three-week assignment that required his expertise. Before he could do his part, a
Turk had to finish another part of the project first. Before leaving the United States Jerry was assured that everything would be
ready for him.

Jerry arrived in Ankara during the first week of December, eager
to do his part. He was hoping to be home for Christmas to spend
it with his wife and newborn baby. To his dismay he found that
a Turk named Ali had not started the project and was nowhere
in sight. In discussing the situation with Ali's boss, he received
no straight answer, just a shrug of the shoulders and a smile. He
could not believe this was happening to him. Seeing no other
choice, he set out to do Ali's part, realizing that Christmas would
be spent in Ankara instead of at home.

He finished Ali's part of the project in two days. As he was finally
starting his part of the project, Ali appeared, ready to work. Jerry
could not understand Ali's calm and undisturbed demeanor, as if
nothing had happened.

Can you make sense of Ali's actions?

1. Ali was the boss's favorite, and he knew that his irresponsibility
   would be tolerated.

2. Ali resented an American being sent to Turkey to do a small
   part of the project.

3. Ali's boss had neglected to tell Ali about the time requirement
   for the job.

4. Ali did not consider two days as a significant delay.

21   I'LL BE HOME FOR CHRISTMAS

1. There is nothing in this incident to indicate this to be the case. Please choose again.

2. Ali could be feeling this way. Turks are a proud people. In this case, however, Jerry's expertise was obviously needed. There is a better answer. Please choose again.

3. This is probably not the case because if Ali's boss had neglected to tell Ali about the time requirement, he would have corrected it when Jerry talked with him. Please choose again.

4. This is the best answer and brings out a point that causes Americans one of their greatest challenges in adjusting to Turkey: the use of time. Americans value time highly. Schedules, as well as vacations, are carefully planned out. Punctuality is adhered to and demanded. In Turkey, on the other hand, there is a more relaxed attitude toward punctuality. On the job, strict deadlines are not seen in the same light by Turks as by Americans. This can cause problems. Turks value not only getting the job done, but just as much, what they gain personally in the process.

22   A MERE TECHNICALITY

Beth was assigned to her company's Turkish plant to build an electrical machinery shop identical to the one that she had assembled in the United States. She was very excited about going to Turkey. Soon after Beth arrived in Ankara she started to train her crew. It seemed to her that the male trainees hesitated to ask her questions even if she was sure that they did not understand her explanations. Beth was careful about her language, especially the technical terms. She would not speak in complicated sentences, but found it difficult to consistently explain things in elementary English. In order to simplify matters, Beth decided not to explain the reason behind a method, and focused primarily on implementation. Several months after her arrival she started feeling that her trainees were not very enthusiastic about her sessions.

Why were the trainees not very enthusiastic about Beth's classes?

1. The Turkish workers would have learned more had Beth told them about the "why", along with the "how."

2. The Turkish workers resented having a woman train them.

3. The trainees started questioning Beth's technical competency.

4. They felt insulted because Beth was talking to them in broken English.

5. The trainees were disgusted with the plodding pace of the training.

22   A MERE TECHNICALITY

1. This is a good explanation since Turks want to know the reasons behind what is being taught. Dealing with proprietary information is a difficult issue. If you are not at liberty to explain something, take time to deal with the Turks' concerns. Choose again for a more important point.

2. This may be true. The roles of the sexes in Turkish society are in a stage of transition, but Turkey remains largely a male dominated culture. As compared with Middle Eastern countries, however, women are much more prevalent and accepted members of the work force. Please choose again.

3. It might appear that Beth does not know the material in depth due to her choice of language, but the incident does not indicate that she could not respond to questions or demonstrate the technology. There is a better answer so please choose again.

4. It is demeaning to be addressed in "baby English." Beth is doing it as a natural response to a difficult situation. Speaking a language is usually the last stage of learning it, therefore, the Turks probably understand more than Beth realizes. If someone cannot speak English fluently, it does not mean that he/she is not a capable and intelligent person. Beth might consider using normal spoken English supplemented with more handouts, drawings, and other visual aids. This is the best answer.

5. This could be true, but there is no way to know for sure. This is a challenge many Americans face. How does one know at what pace to proceed when one is not sure how much the Turks are comprehending? There is a better choice. Please choose again.

23   A RATINGS WAR

Stan was the Vice President of a joint venture company in İzmir,
and 24 Turks were under his supervision. It was time for the
first performance rating. Stan was pleased that 18 of the workers
merited an "excellent" rating and only six placed below that, but
still in the "very good" range. He was impressed by the knowledge and skill of the Turks. He announced the ratings at their
next department meeting. Stan felt tension at the meeting and
attributed it to review jitters. The next day, all six Turks who
had received ratings below "excellent" quit their jobs. Stan was
stunned at losing one-fourth of his department.

What is the most probable reason for the Turks' resignations?

1. The Turks felt that Stan had high expectations, and it would
   only be a matter of time before they would be fired.

2. The six did not feel that the ratings were fair and quit in protest.

3. Stan's critique in front of their co-workers was unacceptable to
   the six Turks.

4. Scaled performance ratings are not an accepted part of Turkish
   business practice.

23   A RATINGS WAR

1. This is not a likely reason since the ratings of the six were in the "very good" range. Please choose again.

2. This is a possible answer, but there is a better cultural explanation of what happened. Please choose again.

3. Turks are generally not as direct as Americans. Stan was handling the situation according to American cultural values rather than finding out what was appropriate in Turkey. In Turkey, people's feelings and relationships are considered important, and a person is usually not criticized in front of his/her peers. Criticism should be indirectly approached, couched in positive terms. It is also better accepted if a good relationship has been developed first. This is the best answer.

4. This approach is not liked in Turkey because it is too direct and does not take people's feelings into account. Even if scaled ratings were to be used, a better approach would be a personal and confidential meeting with each employee. This would permit a greater degree of tact, indirectness, and face saving. Please choose again for a better answer.

24   THE REPORT

Bob was working in İstanbul. He enjoyed living there and was learning a lot about Turkey, but also knew he was there to get the job done. One day he called one of his workers, Osman, to his office and asked him when he could have the production report. Osman said it would take about three days to complete. Bob said that it would be fine. The three days came and went. Bob called Osman in again and asked him where the report was. Osman said that it was not finished because he needed some information from Hikmet, a co-worker in another department, and Hikmet was very busy. Bob could not understand why Osman did not pressure Hikmet to provide the information.

Can you give the most likely reason?

1. Osman was using Hikmet as an excuse.

2. Osman had a looser time concept for the three day deadline.

3. Osman considers his friendship with Hikmet to be more important than meeting the deadline.

4. Osman was teaching his pushy American boss a lesson in patience.

24   THE REPORT

1. Placing the blame on a co-worker would contradict the value placed on friendships. There is a more plausible reason. Please choose again.

2. This is a good answer. As compared with the United States deadlines in Turkey carry a more flexible time concept. Therefore, Osman may not consider the report as late. Please choose again for a more relevant answer.

3. This is the most likely reason. Relationships are often more important than the job at hand. In addition, one's loyalty to the peer group usually takes precedence over individual gain. Osman would rather take the blame than to implicate Hikmet.

4. This could be a possible reason if Bob were not liked by Osman and had not taken the time to establish a relationship with him. Osman, however, is probably acting in this manner for reasons other than to frustrate Bob. Please select another response.

25   AN EXCELLENT FOREMAN

Before leaving the United States to work on a joint venture project
in Turkey, Ben had been told that the Turks with whom he would
be dealing would all be English speaking. When he arrived in
İstanbul, he found their English to be simple and by no means
fluent. He was angry at the home office for misleading him, but
decided to make the best of it. He spoke louder and slower to the
Turks, sometimes using short phrases, instead of complete sentences. This took a lot of time and energy on his part, but he was
determined to make the project a success. In the United States
he was always considered an excellent foreman. To his dismay,
though, the harder he worked at making himself understood, the
more the Turks withdrew from him. He started questioning his
technical competency and self-worth.

How can you help Ben better cope with the situation?

1. Ben should speak at a normal pace avoiding slang and idioms.

2. Ben should use an interpreter for technical discussions.

3. Ben should continue using simple English and non-verbal ges-
   tures.

4. In view of the cross-cultural settings Ben needs to reassess his
   expectations.

25   AN EXCELLENT FOREMAN

1. This would be of help in this situation. Slang and idioms are a difficult part of a language, and by being aware of this fact, and speaking normally, the training would probably go better. However, this may not offer a complete solution to Ben's problem. Please choose again.

2. This is only a temporary solution because it would not help the Turks learn the needed vocabulary. Please choose again.

3. This may be insulting to the Turks and could just make the situation worse. Please choose again.

4. In many foreign assignments, it is impossible to feel and be as competent as one would be at home, due to the cultural and language differences. Assessing what can realistically be accomplished is important in maintaining one's self-image and satisfaction. This is the best answer.

26   A SMILE AND A NOD

Jack was working on a project that his company had with a Turkish firm in İzmir. He was a supervisor and wanted the project to
be a success. One day as he was doing a quality control check, he
discovered that Mehmet had not been doing his work according
to the specifications. Jack was sensitive to the hierarchy structure
at the plant and went to Mehmet's boss, Haluk. He explained the
problem to Haluk and told him that Mehmet had to be confronted
immediately. Haluk smiled and nodded, indicating that he understood what Jack had said. A few days later, Jack discovered that
Mehmet was continuing to disregard the specifications. Jack was
furious but upon approaching Haluk again, just got a smile and
a nod of the head. Jack threw up his hands in despair.

How would you explain the situation to Jack?

1. Although Haluk informed Mehmet of Jack's complaints, Mehmet was a problem employee who had difficulty following in-
   structions.

2. Haluk had a different concept about the appropriate production
   tolerances and ignored Jack's complaints as being too picky.

3. Mehmet obviously had influence with someone of higher authority, therefore Haluk could do nothing.

4. Haluk did not want to jeopardize his working relationship with
   his subordinate by confronting Mehmet directly.

26   A SMILE AND A NOD

1. There is nothing in the situation to indicate this to be the case. Please choose again.

2. Standards of quality can differ from culture to culture, as they can from company to company or worker to worker. As a supervisor, however, Haluk would probably have a better appreciation for the importance of production standards. Consequently, there is a better answer, so please choose again.

3. The hierarchical structure is very much adhered to and if Mehmet has a personal contact higher up, Haluk would bow to that, even though he would resent it. We are not given any indication of this being the case, however. Please choose again.

4. Once more we see where indirectness is the course of behavior. The relationship is very important, and Haluk will ultimately address the problem carefully and tactfully. This slow, considered course of action may bother action oriented Americans. This is the best answer. A better approach for Jack would have been to explain the problem to Haluk, enlisting his help, rather than dictating the required course of action.

27   THE JOB INTERVIEW

Ali was being considered for a job with an American company in Ankara. John, the head of the department, interviewed Ali and asked him about his qualifications. John was surprised at Ali's extreme uneasiness in putting forth his qualifications. Ali's friend Mehmet, who worked with John, had told John about Ali's excellent education and work record. John was hesitant to hire Ali.

Can you help John understand Ali's behavior?

1. Mehmet had exaggerated Ali's qualifications so that his friend would get the job.

2. Ali was a shy person and could not open up in the first meeting.

3. Although Ali had excellent qualifications, his poor English prevented him from presenting them.

4. It is not considered proper to tout one's accomplishments.

27   THE JOB INTERVIEW

1. There is nothing in the scenario to indicate that this is the case. Please choose again.

2. This could be true particularly in the context of a first meeting, but there is a better cultural reason. Please choose again.

3. There is no indication that English proficiency is a problem. Please choose again.

4. Turks place high value on being modest about their accomplishments, and expect employers to find out about them indirectly, through friends, former professors, or former employers. Ali's resume would also be more modestly written than an American one. This is the best answer. This value may be slowly changing, especially in job interviews.

28   THE PICNIC

Frank was living in İzmir where he worked as the quality control manager for a chemical production company. After an intensive personnel selection process, he hired three Turkish women as inspectors. It was their job to inspect the work of a department and to prepare performance reports on every step of the process in that department. Frank was very pleased with the work of the women; their reports were complete, to the point, and accurate. He was proud of having selected the right people for the job, since he had not had much luck in the past. Other inspectors had not written the kind of reports Frank had insisted upon.

One Sunday, the Turkish workers were having a picnic, and Frank was happy to attend. He loved to be a part of the relaxed atmosphere, and enjoyed the good Turkish food, baklava being his favorite. He also liked watching the folk dances that the men performed from various regions of Turkey. Frank noticed that the three women inspectors were not at the picnic. He wondered how anyone could miss such an event!

What is the most probable reason for the absence of the three women inspectors?

1. The workers did not invite them because of the unfavorable reports that they had written.

2. No women were invited to the picnic since Islam requires the separation of sexes.

3. They did not attend, because, as inspectors, they felt that they were above the regular production workers.

4. They were not invited because the male workers resented women in a position of authority.

28   THE PICNIC

1. The women were being direct in their reports, and thereby not adhering to Turkish norms and values. They were showing their co-workers in a bad light. This is the best answer.

2. Turkey is a secular state and therefore not governed by the rules of Islam. Although not required by law, very devout Moslems might practice separation of the sexes on some occasions, but the women would still be in separate attendance. There is a better answer. Please choose again.

3. This could be correct, since hierarchy plays a part in determining with whom one associates. It is, however, not the best answer since Frank was included in the invitation, and he ranks above the inspectors. Please choose again.

4. This is a good answer, because Turkey generally is a male dominated society. However, educated professional women also represent an important group accepted in the workplace. Please choose again for a better answer.

29   A MOVER AND SHAKER

Rich Meyer, a successful manager, was assigned to head the Quality Control Division of the new project that his company had undertaken with a Turkish company in Ankara. He was a great planner and organizer. He also had a reputation of being a mover and shaker and was chosen to replace the Turkish manager. He knew how to motivate people and get the job done. The department in Ankara was behind schedule, and Rich was concerned about it.

During his first week on the job, Rich quickly spotted the reasons for the problem. People spent time visiting and drinking tea for longer than he felt was necessary. Personal conversations were interspersed in discussions of the job. Rich called the department together. In the meeting he said that he wanted people to deal with only business matters during working hours. He asked them to save the socializing and the personal conversations for after-work hours. As an incentive, he offered a bonus for production exceeding the quota. At the end of his second quarter, there were still some small problems, but his division was ahead of schedule. He, therefore, was shocked upon learning that 25 percent of the machine parts that his department approved for quality were later proven to be faulty.

What was the reason for the poor quality control?

1. The Turkish workers resented having an American manager.

2. The workers were sacrificing quality to earn an incentive bonus.

3. The Turkish workers responded to the reduction in social time with a corresponding reduction in job performance.

4. The quality control workers were reluctant to reject poor workmanship to avoid placing their production worker "friends" in a bad light.

29   A MOVER AND SHAKER

1. It is plausible that the Turkish workers resented Rich's replace-
    ment of the Turkish manager, but Rich's production problems
    are probably more attributable to management style. Please
    choose again.

2. Since economic conditions are harsh for many people in Turkey
    this may seem plausible. In Turkish culture, however, honesty
    is as important as financial rewards. There is a better answer.
    Please choose again.

3. Since Rich was ignorant of the Turkish manner of working
    which includes socializing with colleagues, the workers found a
    way of compensating for this by poor work performance. This
    is the best answer.

4. Friendship is not the issue here because the quality control peo-
    ple were rejecting "their friends' work" on even a greater scale
    under the direction of the Turkish manager. Please choose
    again.

30   RED TAPE

Joe Martin wanted to hire a Turk to expedite the paperwork in
the government offices for his company's Turkish branch. He ran
an advertisement in Hürriyet, a prominent daily newspaper. After
an extensive interviewing process he hired Veli, a young Turk who
spoke fluent English and seemed to understand the workings of
the Turkish bureaucracy. Feeling confident that Veli was the right
person for the job, Joe returned to the United States.

A few months later Joe received the quarterly progress report
from his manager in Turkey. The report indicated that they were
falling behind schedule because the permits were still delayed. Joe
called Veli and asked him for an explanation. Veli said that everything was going well and that he was finalizing the arrangements.
Joe was upset and emphasized the importance of adhering to the
schedule.

The following month, Joe called his Turkish branch manager and
inquired about the status of the permits. After learning that they
had still not been issued, Joe became furious. The guy was lying
and giving him the runaround. He told his secretary to prepare a
letter terminating Veli's employment.

Why were the government permits delayed?

1. Joe and Veli each had different concepts of the degree of
   progress that had been achieved.

2. Veli had exaggerated his credentials and his ability to successfully deal with Turkish bureaucracy.

3. Veli was using the slow pace of handling business in government
   offices as an excuse for his lack of success.

4. Everyone involved, including Veli, underestimated the time required to obtain the government permits.

30   RED TAPE

1. Since Veli appears to be a competent person with knowledge of the workings of the government bureaucracy, this seems to be the best answer. Joe Martin is not familiar with the way things are done in Turkey and is using American time guidelines to judge the situation. Since Veli reported that things are proceeding well, it appears that they are seeing progress from different perspectives. Many times schedules are set in the United States for work to be done in Turkey, that are not realistic. This seems to be the case here.

2. Joe Martin had spent a good deal of time in making sure that he selected the right person for the job. This, therefore, is not a good choice. Please choose again.

3. There is no indication in the story that this is true. For a better answer, please choose again.

4. This could be the case, because it is hard to judge exactly how long paperwork takes for any given project. Veli did not indicate this to Joe in their phone conversation, because that would make his judgment appear faulty, and he would be reluctant to admit his error. There is a better answer, however, please choose again.

31   THE VISITING PROFESSOR

Professor Green was teaching at a university in İstanbul as a Fulbright Visiting Professor. İstanbul enthralled him with its scenic beauty and history, yet its European flair. He also enjoyed his apartment on the Bosphorus, with all the amenities of home plus a kapıcı (door man) to run his errands and maintain the building. In particular, the kapıcı would pay Professor Green's bills for him by going to the appropriate offices and paying in cash. Payments in cash were necessary because checking accounts were not widely used.

He was confused when some of the students in his Calculus class returned similar answers to a homework assignment. He became even more irritated when he saw the solutions that the students submitted for a quiz. Some were again very similar. How could this be? He then remembered that he had left the class during the exam after distributing the quiz. He was upset and wanted to do something about this. After all, cheating required severe punishment in the United States.

How can you explain the key cultural difference here to Professor Green?

1. Since other professors did not object, the Turkish students became accustomed to cheating.

2. Competition is so intense that the students in Turkey are forced to cheat.

3. The students view the process more as helping their friends than as cheating.

4. Turkish professors do not leave the room during an exam.

31   THE VISITING PROFESSOR

1. Cheating is not acceptable to professors in Turkey, just as in the United States. Please choose again.

2. This is usually not the case in Turkey and does not address a key cultural point. Please choose again.

3. In Turkish culture the group tends to be more important than the individual. Turkish students may often work together and help each other with their homework. This may extend to the test situation as well. It is not seen as cheating, but rather as helping a friend. This is an important cultural point and is the best answer.

4. This is correct because they are aware of a Turkish cultural value that would prompt what Americans consider "cheating." Please choose again to learn about this value.

32   CLEARING THE AIR

Mike was an effective manager for his company in the United States. Because of this, he was sent to Turkey for a construction project. Mike had been told that Turks were not as time and schedule oriented as Americans, and he had taken that into account. What caught him completely by surprise, however, was how the Turks referred to their co-workers as "friends." For example, they would give reasons for not getting something finished as not wanting to bother a "friend." When Mehmet gave this reason to Mike for not finishing an important report by the deadline, Mike exploded and told him that it was not an acceptable reason and that he had better cut out this "friend" stuff, or else. Mehmet became silent, walked out without saying a word, and avoided Mike thereafter. Mike felt it had been good to clear the air and let Mehmet know how he felt, yet Mehmet became a worker Mike could no longer relate to.

What would explain Mehmet's reaction to Mike's reprimand?

1. Mehmet was angry because he was covering up his co-worker's shortcomings and was not responsible for the delay.

2. Mehmet interpreted Mike's words as a rejection of the personal relationship between them.

3. Mehmet viewed Mike's reaction as an attack on an important Turkish value.

4. Mehmet was insulted by Mike's direct and explosive personal attack.

32   CLEARING THE AIR

1. Friendship is important in Turkey, and Mehmet would probably try to cover up for a friend. Although he might be offended by Mike's reaction, there is nothing in the incident to indicate that Mehmet was angry. Please choose again.

2. Although it would have helped matters if Mike had established a personal working relationship with Mehmet, the incident does not indicate that such a relationship yet existed. Please choose again.

3. The relevant Turkish cultural value is friendship. Establishing a personal relationship is important even in business dealings. Mehmet probably viewed Mike's reaction as belittling this value. This is the best answer. See explanation 4 for another cultural point.

4. This is a good answer. Mike's explosion was too direct a reprimand in a culture which values indirect measures and face saving. This, however, is not the main cultural value in the episode. Please choose again for a better answer.

33   KURBAN BAYRAMI

Fatma had been working as a secretary for Tom Easton for two months. Tom was pleased with her work. They were like a team. In particular, Fatma had been completing her tasks on time.

It was two days before Kurban Bayramı, an important religious holiday. That morning the kapıcı (doorman) and the bekçi (night watchman) for his building arrived at his door and shook his hand. He had heard that he should tip them due to the approaching holiday, and he did so. Tom then left for work.

Tom asked Fatma to get a report from another section of the company before the holiday. By 2 PM of the next day Tom realized that he still had not received the report. He immediately went to see Fatma and found her talking and laughing with other workers. He said, "I see that you spend your time talking with your friends instead of working. Now I understand why you did not get the report to me on time!" He then left. When Tom saw Fatma's resignation letter on his desk after the holiday, he was shocked.

How could Tom have handled the situation better?

1. Tom should have monitored the status of the report more closely with Fatma and thereby avoided the confrontation altogether.

2. Tom should not have reprimanded Fatma in front of her friends.

3. Tom should not have waited until shortly before a major holiday.

4. Tom should have obtained the facts from Fatma in private.

33   KURBAN BAYRAMI

1. As a manager it was not Tom's job to closely monitor the status of a short-term task that he had placed in the hands of a capable secretary. Please choose again.

2. The peer group is important, and Tom made Fatma lose face by reprimanding her in front of her co-workers. This is a good answer, but please choose again for a more complete explanation.

3. Just as the time before Christmas is very busy for most Americans, the same is true for Turks before their major holidays. We do not know, however, if Tom could have avoided this last minute request. Please choose again.

4. Tom made two mistakes, one practical and one cultural. First, he failed to ask Fatma why the report was delayed. Fatma had to obtain the report from another section of the company, and that section might have been the problem. Second, even if Fatma had not performed her duties properly, the public reprimand made Fatma lose face in front of her friends. This is the best answer.

34   A POSTER FOR ALİ BEY

Sylvia wanted to give a New Year's present to her boss, Ali Bey (Bey is a title used for men after the first name and corresponds to Mr. in English). She thought that this would be a good opportunity to show him that she liked Turkey and the Turkish people. She started to look for a poster to frame as a gift for Ali Bey. She bought a picture of two village women in traditional dresses, framed it nicely, and hung it in Ali Bey's office the next morning before he came in. She was really excited about the present.

When Ali Bey saw the picture, he stopped for a few seconds and said, "Thank you." Two days later, when Sylvia did not see the picture, she felt offended and asked him about it. His answer was, "I really liked the picture, and I wanted to share it with my family, so I took it home."

Why do you think Ali Bey took the picture home?

1. Ali Bey resented Sylvia deciding what should go in his office.

2. Ali Bey did not like having a picture of women on his wall.

3. Ali Bey indeed liked the poster, but felt that it was more appropriate for his home than his office.

4. Ali Bey was hurt that the picture was Sylvia's image of Turkey.

34   A POSTER FOR ALİ BEY

1. Ali Bey probably felt that his office was his private space. Sylvia should not have imposed by hanging her present on the office wall. There is a better answer, however, please choose again.

2. It is hard to know what his personal taste would be, so this is possible. However, although he did not like the picture particularly, he probably would have kept it on the wall somewhat longer to be polite. There is a cultural point involved. Please choose again.

3. Ali Bey's response was an indirect and tactful way of telling Sylvia that the picture was not appropriate for his office. Please choose again.

4. Turks are sensitive to how their country is perceived. They want to be seen as European; to have their modern buildings and bridges appreciated. Sylvia was showing him that she saw his country as typified by poor village women. Americans view village scenes as interesting and colorful, whereas Turks may see it as being thought of as poor and backward. In addition, Sylvia had placed the picture in Ali Bey's office where it would be viewed by his most important and influential business associates. In view of the circumstances he could not politely permit it to remain for even a few days. This is the best answer.

35 WASHING UP

John was assigned to work in Kayseri for two years on a project between his employer and a Turkish company. One Friday, toward noon, he walked into the big bathroom at work. To his dismay, an older worker was washing his feet in one of the sinks. John was disturbed by the sight.

Why do you think the worker was washing his feet in the sink?

1. The worker was preparing himself for prayer.

2. He probably did not have hot running water at home.

3. Turks wash both their hands and their feet before they eat.

4. His feet were dirty, and he was simply washing them off.

35   WASHING UP

1. Friday noon is the most important prayer time for Moslems. One requirement for prayer is to first wash parts of one's head, arms, and feet. The worker was probably pèrforming this ritual, called "abdest." This is the best answer.

2. This is possible because hot running water is a luxury for many people. That does not fully explain why he was washing his feet, and there is a more likely answer. Please choose again.

3. This is not a correct answer. Please choose again.

4. Depending on the work he does, this could be true. There is a better answer. Please choose again.

C. In Public

Are we still having fun?
There is a better answer.
Please choose again!

36   WELCOME

Linda was joining her husband to live in İstanbul for a two year
assignment. Bill had arrived two months earlier and had written
to her about Turkey, the people and customs. He had told her
about the hospitality of the Turks. She was anxious to see Bill
again and to start her new life.

She got off the plane and proceeded through customs with her
two large suitcases. As she left customs she looked for Bill, but
before she knew it, she saw two men quickly approaching her.
They looked menacing and determined, and scared her such that
she dropped her bags, covered her face, and screamed, bracing
herself for the attack she thought was imminent.

What is the most probable explanation for the Turks' actions?

1. The Turks were rushing to help Linda since they saw her strug-
   gling with her bags.

2. The Turks wanted to steal her bags since she was alone.

3. The Turks were taxi drivers and were trying to get Linda's
   business.

4. Bill was delayed at work, and he sent them to meet her.

36   WELCOME

1. Turks are hospitable people, and therefore this is a possibility. There is a better answer. Please choose again.

2. It is highly unlikely that anyone would attempt to steal such bulky items at a busy airport. Please choose again.

3. Turkish taxi drivers sometimes approach potential customers and try to carry their luggage toward their taxis. They have found this to be an effective way of getting business. This is the best answer.

4. It is unlikely that Bill would send strangers to welcome his wife after a significant period of separation and on her first trip to a foreign country. Please choose again.

37   AT THE RESTAURANT

Mike and Dan were working on a technology transfer project in Ankara. One day they decided to run out to a nearby Turkish restaurant for lunch. They ordered some sigara böreği (filled fluffy pastry rolls), kuru fasulye (beans), and İzmir köfte (meatballs and potatoes in a gravy) and a bottle of Kavaklıdere wine.

The meal came quickly, and they enjoyed the delicious flavors and felt good about frequenting a local restaurant filled with Turks. They finished their meal and chatted while waiting for the check. Minutes passed. They became impatient and glanced in the direction of the garson (waiter). He was standing nearby, talking to another waiter, occasionally glancing at them. Finally, in disgust, they started to get up and leave, to show their disapproval of the service. The garson came running after them, waving the check.

Can you explain to Mike and Dan why the check was not presented earlier?

1. In Turkey, it is considered impolite to present the check before being summoned.

2. The waiter wanted to keep the Americans in the restaurant as long as possible, hoping that they would order more food and drink.

3. The waiter was more interested in talking to the other waiter than in doing his job.

4. Once more, as Americans, Mike and Dan were the victims of bad service abroad.

37   AT THE RESTAURANT

1. In Turkey, once the meal is served, a good waiter does not approach the table until summoned. The waiter was acting properly by not inquiring about how the food was or by presenting the check without being asked. This is the best answer.

2. This is improbable; if he wanted to do this, he would have offered them other menu suggestions. Please choose again.

3. It is natural for a person to be involved in short personal conversations on the job in Turkey, and this does not indicate that he was not doing his job. Please choose again.

4. This is an easy conclusion to jump to whenever a situation is not understood. It is not the case here. Please choose again.

38   NO PROBLEM

Bob had recently accepted a job in İstanbul. He and his wife, Linda, wanted to find a suitable grade school for their two children. They had heard about the American Community School in İstanbul where the classes were being taught in English, and most of the teachers were native English speakers.

They took a taxi from their hotel and asked the driver if he knew the location of the school. The driver said, "No problem." After more than an hour of driving they suspected that the driver was lost. He stopped several times, shook his head, and spoke to people on the street.

What is the most plausible explanation for the driver's behavior?

1. He was trying to inflate the fare by pretending that he did not know the directions.

2. The driver thought that he knew the directions but later realized that he was mistaken.

3. He did not know the exact location of the school, but it was important to him to appear capable.

4. The driver did not want to admit that he did not know the directions, because he was afraid that he would lose the fare.

38   **NO PROBLEM**

1. If he were trying to purely inflate the fare, he would not be stopping and talking with people and shaking his head. There is a better reason. Please choose again.

2. This could happen, but it is not the main cultural point. Please choose again.

3. The driver was probably trying to "save face." A person in Turkey may not want to admit that he does not know something. "No problem," can sometimes mean exactly the opposite. This is the best answer.

4. It is obviously important for the driver to have customers, but there is a cultural point that is more relevant. Please choose again.

39   CALIFORNIA GIRL

Karen decided to do the shopping herself rather than having the kapıcı (doorman) do it. She had heard about the open market that was held every Saturday in Beşiktaş. Karen was a real California girl and loved to feel comfortable in the summer with light clothing. It was a hot summer day so she wore her Hawaiian shorts and a matching halter top. The brightly colored outfit went very well with her long blonde hair. When she walked by the coffee-house she saw men rushing to the windows to watch her pass by. She could hear them exclaiming, "Maşallah!" (God Protect!)

At the open market it was even worse. The market was very busy and noisy, and Karen felt pushed, shoved, and elbowed as she tried to make her way through the crowd. She saw many women with scarves on their heads. Once more she became aware that men were staring at her, and women seemed to be whispering about her. Karen began to feel increasingly uncomfortable and decided to go home. She was not sure if she wanted to learn about the city or its people.

Why were the Turks reacting to Karen in this manner?

1. Karen's long blonde hair, which she wore loose, caused the attention she received.

2. It is very unusual for women to go to the open market alone.

3. Wearing shorts and a halter top in public is not acceptable.

4. Although wearing shorts and a halter top would be acceptable in cities, the bright colors are not appropriate.

39   CALIFORNIA GIRL

1. Although her long blonde hair would attract attention, it is only one factor. Please choose again.

2. It is acceptable for a woman to go to the open market alone. Please choose again.

3. Karen's dress was not appropriate for anyplace but perhaps a tourist beach or certain parts of big cities. In an open market the people selling the produce come in from the villages, where standards of dress and behavior are more conservative than in the cities. This is the best answer. A woman walking on the street should not smile, look at, or talk to a strange man. Any of those things could be construed as invitations by the woman, especially if she is a foreigner. American women are often stereotyped by Turks as "available" because of television programs such as Dallas and Dynasty, which are seen in Turkey.

4. Karen's attire would only be acceptable in certain places such as a tourist beach in Turkey. Americans tend to wear brighter colors than Turks, and may draw attention to themselves because of it. There is, however, a better explanation. Please choose again.

40   THE FUSSY BUYERS

Jim and Carol were newlyweds. They had recently arrived in Turkey for a project on which Jim was working. Mahmut, a co-worker, had offered to take them shopping for Turkish rugs.

As they went from store to store, Jim and Carol walked with their arms around one another while talking with Mahmut. They teased each other playfully while sitting in the rug shops. Although they had visited a number of shops, Jim and Carol were unable to select a rug to their liking. Mahmut became increasingly quiet and suggested visiting one more shop. Jim and Carol, however, politely declined the suggestion, noting their fatigue as the reason. The next day, at work, Mahmut seemed to avoid any contact with Jim.

What was the most probable reason for Mahmut's behavior?

1. Mahmut was offended by Jim and Carol's public display of physical affection.

2. Mahmut felt excluded by the undivided attention that Jim and Carol displayed for each other in the rug shops.

3. Mahmut thought that Jim and Carol had wasted his time and were not really interested in purchasing a rug.

4. Mahmut felt rejected because Jim and Carol declined his offer to visit another rug store.

40   THE FUSSY BUYERS

1. In Turkey, although there may be some public display of affection between members of the same sex, it is usually not
   acceptable between members of opposite sexes. For example,
   it is customary for men or women to kiss others of the same
   sex on both cheeks as a form of greeting or parting. This is
   the best answer.

2. It is embarrassing for a Turk to be excluded from a group
   outing. On the other hand, the incident states that Jim and
   Carol spoke with Mahmut while walking from store to store,
   and the degree of exclusion may not have been that great.
   Please choose again.

3. Jim and Carol seemed to give that impression, with their complete involvement with each other, so this could be how he felt.
   Please choose again, however, for a better answer.

4. Wanting to help his friends buy a rug of their choice, he may
   have felt disappointed at not being able to take them to another
   store. However, it had not been a good day for Mahmut, and
   he probably was somewhat relieved in seeing it come to an end.
   There is a better answer. Please choose again.

41 MANAV

One morning, Carol decided to buy some fruit from the corner
"manav" (fruit stand). When she arrived at the shop, the merchant was helping another customer. She wanted to buy some
apples and started selecting the green ones from the beautifully
arranged display. She wanted the greener ones because her apartment was warm, and she was afraid that the riper apples would
spoil quickly. The store owner became upset, spoke to her loudly
in Turkish, grabbed her bag, and emptied it. Hurt and confused,
Carol left the store immediately and started to cry.

Can you explain the merchant's actions to Carol?

1. Under Turkish health and sanitation laws, only the merchant
   may handle the food.

2. The merchant was angry because Carol disturbed the neat ar-
   rangement of his display.

3. Carol should not have selected just the green apples.

4. The merchant was upset because it was his job to choose and
   bag the apples.

41   MANAV

1. This is not correct. Please choose again.

2. Merchants take great pride in the beautiful displays they create with their produce. Seeing it disturbed could be part of
   the reason the store owner was upset. For a more complete
   explanation, please choose again.

3. Since fruit and vegetables are usually purchased for immediate
   consumption, Turkish customers generally value ripe produce
   and would not want the green apples. Please choose again.

4. Not only does the merchant arrange the beautiful displays of
   his fruits and vegetables, he also chooses and bags them. He
   does not want the display disturbed and wants to control the
   selection and quality of the produce sold to each customer.
   Developing a good relationship with one's neighborhood merchants can result in their selection of better produce. This is
   the best answer.

42   SOUVENIRS

Brian and Janet had been living in Turkey for about a year. They were preparing for a trip to the United States and wanted to buy some presents for their friends and relatives. One day they went to a local souvenir shop and spotted two photo albums. One of the albums had the Blue Mosque engraved on the cover, and the other had a beautiful picture of the Bosphorus Bridge at sunset. They noticed that the items were very well made but were quite expensive. They heatedly bargained with the merchant, threatening to leave several times, and ultimately paid a greatly reduced price for the albums. Brian felt very smug about his bargaining prowess.

Janet's sister was an avid swimmer so they returned to the shop the next day to purchase a swimsuit, ideally with a Turkish flag motif. Janet's sister was blonde, and the red background of the Turkish flag would complement her hair. Upon entering the shop it was obvious that the merchant recognized them. Janet approached the shop owner and inquired if he carried any swimsuits with such a design. The shop owner became angry and started shouting. Brian and Janet left the store immediately.

What made the merchant so angry?

1. It is not acceptable for a foreigner to wear any form of the Turkish flag.

2. It is insulting to make clothing out of a Turkish flag material.

3. As a devout Moslem, the shopkeeper was insulted by the suggestion that he would carry swimsuits.

4. Brian and Janet's intense bargaining for the photo albums the day before had antagonized the merchant.

42   SOUVENIRS

1. A Turk, in general, would appreciate a foreigner's display of affection for Turkey. An exception to this is explained in the best answer. Please choose again.

2. With the value of the group being placed above that of the individual, comes the value of nationalism and showing respect for the flag, national anthem and Atatürk, above individual freedom to wear what one pleases. Wearing the Turkish flag as clothing in the form of a swimsuit or t-shirt would be considered very insulting. On the other hand, the flag is seen on sports clothing of competition teams, or on small lapel pins, to indicate nationalistic feelings of pride or love for Turkey. This is the best answer.

3. There is nothing in the incident to indicate that the merchant is a devout Moslem. Even if he were a devout Moslem, he might still sell swimsuits. Please choose again.

4. Quite the opposite could be true. Bargaining is considered an art in Turkey, and people who know the art and do it well are respected. Brian seemed to know how to drive a hard bargain, and the merchant gave him the albums at a price he was satisfied with or he would have allowed Brian to leave without them. Please choose again.

43   A BARGAIN AT ANY PRICE

Before coming to Turkey, Alice was told that bargaining was a way of life in Turkey. One day she wanted to purchase a pair of shoes and went to a large store. Alice noticed that the prices were higher than those in other stores. She chose a pair of black leather shoes and tried them on. They looked very nice on her and felt very comfortable. The clerk complimented Alice on her good taste.

She asked the price. The clerk showed her the price tag and told her that it was the price. Alice said, "I know, I saw the tag, but I am talking about your final price." The clerk looked confused. He said, "The price on the tag is the final price madam. There is no bargaining in this store." Now Alice was confused. She told the clerk that she knew Turkish customs, and that nobody would buy anything without bargaining.

Why was Alice confused?

1. In certain stores the government regulates the prices, and bargaining is not allowed.

2. The clerk was offended because Alice did not know the etiquette of bargaining.

3. Bargaining was allowed in the store, but the clerk thought that he could take advantage of a foreigner.

4. Some stores do not allow bargaining.

43   A BARGAIN AT ANY PRICE

1. The government does regulate the prices of certain items such as bread, sugar, and paper. The prices of some other items such as clothing and shoes, however, are not regulated. Please choose again.

2. Bargaining is an art in Turkey, but not knowing how to do it properly is not the issue here. Please choose again.

3. There is a better cultural explanation. Moreover, the clerk may be on a fixed salary and would have nothing to gain. Please choose again.

4. It is true that bargaining is very prevalent in Turkey, but as in this case, there are exceptions. Stores that display prices, in general, do not allow bargaining. In smaller and owner-operated stores, it is more likely that bargaining is appropriate. This is the best answer.

44   CHRISTMAS SHOPPING

Frank and Mary had just moved to İstanbul. They had heard so much in the United States about the Grand Bazaar (Kapalı Çarşı) that they decided to do their Christmas shopping there. The next day at work, Frank mentioned their plans to a co-worker, Ahmet. He asked for the directions to the jewelry section and whether or not he should try to bargain. Ahmet indicated that it would be better if they were accompanied by a Turk and offered to go with them. Frank wished that he had not said anything since he did not know what to make of Ahmet's offer.

Why did Ahmet offer to help?

1. Ahmet knew jewelers at the Grand Bazaar and would receive a commission from them.

2. Ahmet was showing Turkish hospitality.

3. Ahmet wanted special treatment from Frank at work.

4. Ahmet expected to be paid as a guide if he took them out.

44   CHRISTMAS SHOPPING

1. It could be that Ahmet knows some jewelers, since people are not as mobile in Turkey and deal with the same family for generations. It is not likely, however, that he would offer to help in order to get a commission. Please choose again.

2. Some Americans have a hard time getting used to Turkish hospitality, because it is a new concept for them. Turks go out of their way to help foreign guests in their country. Their hospitality is a point of national pride. This is the best answer.

3. Given the Turkish culture, this is not a likely answer. Please choose again.

4. There are people who can be hired to be guides on sightseeing or shopping trips, and they do it for pay. An offer by a co-worker would generally not carry the expectation of payment in return. Please choose again.

45   SIGHTSEEING IN İSTANBUL

Orhan took his friends Jim and Janice for a sightseeing tour of İstanbul. He was very anxious to show his American guests the museums, famous mosques, modern buildings, beautiful parks, and the two new suspension bridges across the Bosphorus linking Europe and Asia.

While passing the Grand Bazaar, Jim and Janice started taking pictures of old merchants, shoeshine boys, and the porters carrying heavy loads on their backs. They realized that Orhan was not very eager to join them. He told them to save their film for the beautiful places that they had yet to see. Janice was really attracted to the pigeons in front of the mosque they were passing. She soon started taking pictures of the people leaving the mosque. Orhan approached Jim and said that he had to leave for a business appointment that he had completely forgotten. Although Orhan was very apologetic, Jim and Janice sensed that he was disturbed about something.

How do you interpret the situation?

1. Orhan was hurt because Jim and Janice were ignoring his expertise.

2. Orhan was offended by Jim and Janice's interest in the subjects which portrayed Turkey in a less than favorable light.

3. Orhan was concerned that Janice was photographing the worshipers leaving the mosque.

4. Orhan had indeed forgotten an important business meeting; any offense that he may have taken at Jim and Janice's actions would otherwise be outweighed by his duty to be a good host.

45   SIGHTSEEING IN İSTANBUL

1. It is unlikely that this is the problem. Please choose again.

2. Turks, wanting to be portrayed and appreciated as modern and progressive, can be offended by the attention Americans pay to the parts of Turkish life that do not exhibit this. This is the best answer.

3. This is a good answer. Taking pictures of religious people without their permission may be upsetting to them. For a more comprehensive answer, however, please choose again.

4. It is very unlikely that Orhan would have made plans to be with Jim and Janice, forgetting that a meeting was scheduled. Please choose again for a better answer.

46   CUMHURİYET BAYRAMI

It was the morning of October 29, Cumhuriyet Bayramı, the Turkish Independence Day. Tony Brown was sitting in a jail cell in
İzmir, trying to reconstruct the events of the night before.

The last thing he remembered clearly was arriving at the home
of his friend Tom. Tom had thrown the party for the Americans
in their department, because the next day was a holiday. On his
way to the party he had noticed that the street seemed like a sea
of red, due to the many Turkish flags on buildings, balconies, and
flagpoles. He also had noticed the abundance of wreaths with
laurel leaves surrounding Atatürk's famous statue.

At the party, beer, American liquor, as well as rakı (a popular
clear anisette liquor, which becomes cloudy when mixed with water) flowed freely. He vaguely remembered leaving the party. A
pelting rain was falling as he stumbled down the street toward
his apartment. Suddenly, something wet slapped him in the face.
Terrified, he grabbed it, threw it to the ground, and stomped on
it, thinking that it could be alive. The next thing he knew, he
woke up in the jail cell.

Why was Tony in jail?

1. He was in jail for being drunk in public.

2. Tony had unknowingly assaulted a policeman who was trying
   to help him when he stumbled.

3. He was jailed for treating the Turkish flag in an insulting manner.

4. Tony was arrested for being out after curfew.

46 CUMHURİYET BAYRAMI

1. This is the lesser of the evils he committed that night. Please choose again for a better answer.

2. This would be a good cause for arrest. The incident, however, does not state that this happened. Please choose again.

3. The wet object was most likely the Turkish flag, which is treated with great respect since it symbolizes the Turkish nation. Disrespect shown to the flag can carry grave consequences. Feelings of nationalism are very strong in Turkey, and a foreigner needs to realize this. This is the best answer.

4. There is no mention of a curfew in the incident. Please choose again.

47   TEA FOR TWO

Tony and Carol were living in İstanbul with their five-year old daughter Lisa. Tony was a teacher at Robert College. With Carol's blonde hair and Tony's blue eyes, Lisa was the apple of their eye.

One morning, Tony and Carol were having tea on their balcony while Lisa was playing with a friend in front of their apartment. They became alarmed when they saw a stranger approach the children and pinch Lisa on the cheek and make a funny sound. Tony and Carol were ready to rush out but stopped when they saw the man walk away. They were puzzled by the man's actions.

Why did the man pinch Lisa's cheek?

1. Lisa's blue eyes and blonde hair attracted the attention of the stranger.

2. The children were playing too loudly, and the man was disciplining them.

3. The man was expressing his affection for children.

4. He was wishing the child good luck.

47   TEA FOR TWO

1. Lisa's eyes and hair would attract attention, but this is not the main point. Please choose again.

2. This is a possible conclusion that can be drawn if you are not familiar with the Turkish culture, but it is not the right answer. Please choose again.

3. Turks are family oriented and show great affection for children. One of the unique ways that they display this is by pinching children's cheeks and saying, "Maşallah" (God Protect). Lisa's hair and eyes probably attracted him to pinch her cheek rather than the other child's. This is the best answer.

4. This is partially correct because the funny sound the man uttered was a wish for good luck. Please choose again.

48   RAMAZAN

It was Ramazan, the month of fasting in Turkey. Bill had been in
İstanbul for nine months. He spent much of his free time reading
about Turkey and interacting with Turks. Bill was told that more
than 95 percent of the Turkish people are Moslem. He thought
that he was going to have a difficult time eating openly in public since everybody would be fasting. As a sensitive visitor, he
decided not to eat in public or otherwise in the presence of Turkish people. However, when he saw some of the Turks eating and
smoking, he was shocked. It was even more confusing for him
when he saw some people drinking in a bar.

How would you explain these apparent contradictions to Bill?

1. Bill was observing people from the non-Moslem population, a
   preponderance of whom reside in İstanbul.

2. There is freedom of choice in religious observance since Turkey
   is a secular state.

3. The Turks that he observed were breaking the law, but the
   penalties are not strictly enforced.

4. Fasting takes place only from sunset to sunrise.

48   RAMAZAN

1. It is true that most of the non-Moslem Turks live in İstanbul. It seems, however, too coincidental that Bill came upon such a large segment of the non-Moslem minority. Please choose again.

2. Turkey is a secular state, and during Ramazan people who are religious will adhere strictly to the requirements of fasting, whereas others will not. This is one important difference between Turkey and the other Islamic countries. This is the best answer.

3. Since Turkey is a secular state, there are no laws mandating that Turks fast during Ramazan. Please choose again.

4. Quite to the contrary, fasting takes place from sunrise to sunset. Please choose again.

49   IN THE FAST LANE

Dan was new in Ankara and was learning his way around the city. He noticed that the Turks honked their horns and were more aggressive in their driving than Americans. What really bothered him were the near rear end collisions he had experienced when coming to a complete stop at a red light. He noticed that, occasionally, especially at night, some Turks just slowed down and then proceeded through the intersection against the red light. They seemed upset with him when he did not do the same.

Can you help Dan understand the situation?

1. Under Turkish traffic laws, red lights are treated as caution lights during periods of light traffic.

2. Although running a red light is a traffic violation, some Turks are pragmatic about obeying traffic laws.

3. Turks are aggressive drivers, and they break the law as often as they obey it.

4. Having the reputation of being daring drivers, Turks particularly like to show off their driving skills to foreign visitors.

49   IN THE FAST LANE

1. This is an incorrect answer. Please choose again.

2. In Turkey, passing through a red light is a traffic violation, and a traffic policeman would issue a ticket if he were present. Some people may see it as expeditious not to obey the red light when there is no traffic present. It is important for one to be aware that people drive differently in Turkey than in the United States. Take time to become familiar with the driving patterns before attempting to drive. Taxis are plentiful and reasonably priced and can be a viable alternative to driving. This is the best answer.

3. Driving in Turkey is more difficult and adventurous compared to the United States, but it is incorrect to label Turkish drivers as scofflaws. Please choose again for a better answer.

4. It does not seem plausible that the Turks are driving dangerously simply to impress any foreigners who might be present. Please choose again.

50   ALL DRESSED UP

Sally arrived in İzmir six months ago. She was told that economic
conditions were particularly harsh for low income people. However, she saw few shabby looking persons on the street, and most
people were reasonably well-dressed. She was puzzled with this
contradiction.

How would you explain this to her?

1. People in Turkey generally wear their best in public.

2. Clothing is very inexpensive in Turkey.

3. She lived in the affluent part of town and therefore did not see
   the poor people.

4. Being well-dressed is more important in cities than in the rural
   areas.

50   ALL DRESSED UP

1. A high value is put on appearing at your best in public. Great
   measures are taken not to appear poor. Because of this value,
   the casual attire worn by Americans, such as torn, dirty jeans,
   can be offensive and create a bad first impression. One's ap-
   pearance at a first meeting will greatly determine how that
   person is judged. This is the best answer.

2. In the big cities such as İstanbul, Ankara, and İzmir, the latest
   European fashions are available and can be quite expensive.
   Women in these cities will spend a large percentage of their
   income for clothing. Turkey has a thriving textile industry and
   is famous for its production of leather goods. Turkish made
   clothing would be considered relatively inexpensive by American standards, but maintaining a large wardrobe of fashionable
   clothes would be beyond the means of many Turks. Please
   choose again.

3. People wear their best in public no matter where they live or
   what their economic status is. Please choose again.

4. Being well-dressed is highly valued in all parts of Turkey. Of
   course, what is acceptable and customary clothing will differ in
   an urban setting as compared with a rural atmosphere. Please
   choose again.

51   TWO BEERS

Before coming to Turkey, Steve attended a week-long cross-cultural training program. This program eliminated many of his worries about Turkey. After he had been in Ankara for five months he felt comfortable with the new culture. A recent incident, however, really confused him.

For the last few weeks he had been frequenting a trendy bar in Kızılay after work. Yesterday, before leaving the plant, he met Hasan, a Turkish mechanic in his division. After chatting for a few minutes, Steve invited Hasan to join him for a drink at this new bar. After enjoying two beers, they decided to leave. Hasan picked up the tab and quickly paid. Steve then asked Hasan how much his share was. Looking somewhat irritated, Hasan said that it was not very important. Steve replied "Of course it is, considering how overpaid I am." Hasan said good-bye and left. When they met again the next morning Steve felt that Hasan was not acting in his usual friendly manner.

Can you explain Hasan's behavior?

1. Hasan felt that Steve was boasting by taking him to a trendy bar.

2. Hasan was embarrassed by Steve's reference to their salary discrepancy.

3. Steve's invitation to a bar showed his insensitivity to Hasan's religious beliefs.

4. Hasan was offended by the idea of sharing the bill.

51   TWO BEERS

1. Nothing in the incident indicates that this was a problem for Hasan. Since Steve invited Hasan for drinks, Steve was acting as a hospitable person. Please choose again.

2. This is a good answer, but not the best one. It was insensitive of Steve to bring up how overpaid he was. Americans are usually paid more than their Turkish counterparts. It is important to be aware of this fact. In fairness to Steve, however, he probably made this comment to make Hasan feel better about letting Steve pay his portion of the bill. Steve's comment was probably not interpreted by Hasan in the intended manner, because Steve was unaware of a significant Turkish cultural point. Please choose again.

3. This is not a plausible explanation, because if Hasan were a religious person he would have declined Steve's invitation to visit a bar. Please choose again.

4. There is no concept of "Dutch Treat" in Turkey. Usually, the person who issues the invitation is the one who is expected to pay. Steve invited Hasan. Therefore, if he had been aware of Turkish custom, he should have paid the total bill. Hasan may have rushed to pay the bill because he considered Steve a guest in his country and was extending Turkish hospitality. This is the best answer.

52   LET ME GIVE YOU A TIP

One day Alan decided to go to the Grand Bazaar to buy a present for his wife. With his limited Turkish he asked a shoeshine boy for the location of the nearest bus-stop. To his surprise, the boy responded in broken English and took Alan to the bus station himself. Since it was a ten minute walk, Alan did not understand why he did that instead of just giving the directions. Alan had heard from one of his Turkish friends that tipping is very common in Turkey. He started to wonder whether he should have tipped the boy.

Why did the Turkish boy walk Alan to the bus-stop?

1. The boy expected a big tip from Alan.

2. The boy was displaying Turkish hospitality.

3. The shoeshine boy wanted to practice his limited English with an American.

4. Business was slow, and the boy was happy to find an interesting distraction.

52   LET ME GIVE YOU A TIP

1. Tipping for small services is very common in Turkey, but there is a better answer. Please choose again.

2. Most Americans are surprised by the hospitality that they find afforded them in Turkey. Turks pride themselves on their hospitality and generally expect nothing in return. This is the best answer.

3. Many Turks welcome the opportunity to speak English, but there is a better explanation which raises an important cultural point. Please choose again.

4. Nothing in the incident indicates this. Please choose again.

53   STROLLING IN İSTANBUL

It was Mark's first month in Turkey. One Saturday he set out to see the sights of İstanbul. He first went to Osmanbey, one of the more prosperous and exclusive sections of İstanbul with many fashionable boutiques. He felt very comfortable with the European atmosphere. He then strolled to Şişli, another section of İstanbul. On the street he observed some men walking arm in arm, joking and patting one another on the back. In addition, he observed some men exchanging kisses on the cheeks. Mark felt uncomfortable at the thought of having male friends who would be that "physical" with him.

How would you explain these scenes to Mark?

1. It was the "Şeker Bayramı" (Candy Holiday), and it was customary for men to act in this manner.

2. This is accepted everyday behavior in Turkey.

3. Close family ties are very important for Turks, and these men were probably relatives.

4. Şişli is the area frequented by homosexuals.

53   STROLLING IN İSTANBUL

1. Their behavior does not indicate that it was the Candy Holiday. Please choose again.

2. Turks do not feel uncomfortable with closeness, as compared with most Americans who prefer a greater distance. For example, kissing on both cheeks is a common form of greeting and leave taking. All of the things Mark observed are common ways of relating to people of the same sex. The same behavior is displayed by women. This is the best answer.

3. Close family ties are important, but this behavior would not be confined to relatives. Please choose again.

4. This is not a correct answer. Some Americans misjudge these scenes because of their cultural background. Please choose again.

54   YARDIM

Steve and Mary went to a new restaurant in Kızılay, a central
district of Ankara. The menu was written in Turkish, with de-
scriptive English words in parentheses. The waiter appeared and
asked them if they were ready to order. Steve quickly opened
his Turkish–English dictionary. By pointing to the Turkish word
"yardım" (help) he indicated to the waiter that they needed assistance. He led Steve and Mary to the kitchen and showed them
the day's offerings. Steve and Mary made their choices on the
spot and were very pleased.

During the meal they wanted to order some additional beverages,
but the helpful waiter did not come near them. He did not even
ask them during the meal if they liked their food!

Why was the waiter behaving in this manner?

1. By being shown the kitchen, Steve and Mary became "guests
   of the house" and this made it the restaurant manager's responsibility to serve their table.

2. The waiter was being inattentive.

3. Because the waiter took them to the kitchen for their initial
   order, he expected that they would return to the kitchen if they
   needed further assistance.

4. The waiter was respecting the customers' privacy by standing
   at a distance.

54   YARDIM

1. This is not a custom. Please choose again.

2. By American standards he may appear inattentive, but not so by Turkish standards. Please choose again.

3. This is not the correct answer. Please choose again.

4. In Turkey, it is customary for waiters to keep a distance from customers until summoned. Diners are free to spend as much time over a meal as they choose, and a good waiter does not approach the table. This is the best answer.

55   KAPALI ÇARŞI (THE GRAND BAZAAR)

Ron and Ruth were living in İstanbul because of Ron's job assignment. During the first month there, they wanted to visit the Kapalı Çarşı (Grand Bazaar). They set a Saturday aside from Ron's busy work schedule to buy a Turkish rug for their apartment, as well as some gold jewelry and a leather jacket for Ruth.

As they entered a rug shop, the owner came running toward them, gesturing that they come in and be seated on a low couch. The man spoke no English and ran outside calling to someone. He returned with a young Turkish student who spoke English quite well. Another man entered carrying a tray of small glasses filled with tea, which he placed in front of them. The young man welcomed them to the shop, asked them where they were from, and how they liked Turkey. Ron and Ruth grew increasingly anxious about this waste of time and indicated that they were there to look at Turkish rugs. The student assured them that they would see beautiful rugs from Kayseri, one of the most famous rug regions of Turkey. He encouraged them to relax and enjoy themselves, as he motioned for more tea to be served. By this time, Ron and Ruth had all they could take of the distractions and abruptly walked out. They ignored the student's pleas to return.

Why did the Turks act in this manner?

1. They wanted to make the Americans feel obligated to buy.

2. The Turks wanted to establish a personal relationship first.

3. The Turks were not eager enough to sell them a rug.

4. The Turkish student wanted to practice his English.

55   KAPALI ÇARŞI (THE GRAND BAZAAR)

1. The Turkish merchant of course wanted to sell them a rug. His behavior, however, was dictated by Turkish custom, rather than a product of intentional sales manipulation. Please choose again.

2. In the Turkish culture, personal relationships have a high value, and it is important for Turks to spend time getting to know someone before conducting business. Tea is offered in many places of business, as a gesture of hospitality. Americans may view the young student's questions as too personal or as a waste of time, but the Turks see it as a part of establishing a personal relationship. This is the best answer.

3. This is not a correct answer; on the contrary, their actions indicated that they were eager to do business. Please choose again.

4. This may be true, but it is a minor point. Even if this were the case, the shop owner would not have allowed it to jeopardize a potential sale. Please choose again.

56   TOPKAPI PALACE

Herb was in İstanbul for a day. He had just finished visiting
Topkapı Palace and stopped to get his shoes polished by a curbside
shoeshine boy. After he had his shoes polished, he reached for his
wallet to pay the boy, only to find it missing. Excited and upset,
Herb ran to a policeman standing in front of the Palace. Just
as he was trying to communicate with the policeman, two boys
ran up and handed him his wallet. He immediately checked the
contents of his billfold and found that nothing was missing.

Why did the boys bring Herb his wallet?

1. The boys expected a big reward.

2. They were afraid of being arrested.

3. The boys were afraid of losing their fingers if caught.

4. They were being honest.

56   **TOPKAPI PALACE**

1. Although the boys would probably have appreciated a small tip, this was probably not the motivation for returning the wallet. Please choose again.

2. This could be a natural response, particularly because of the presence of a policeman. There is, however, a more pertinent cultural point. Please choose again.

3. This may be a misconception that some Americans hold about Turkey. Turkey has adopted laws from European penal codes which do no not prescribe such punishments. Please choose again.

4. Honesty is given a high value in Turkey, and the boys were probably displaying this quality. This is the best answer.

57   DON'T HIT MY MERCEDES

Julie wanted to do her shopping while her husband Bill was at work. It was a typical rush hour in İstanbul. After spending half an hour in a traffic jam, Julie was so happy to arrive at the marketplace that she became careless, and a taxi hit the rear bumper of her beautiful Mercedes.

She got out of the car and faced the upset taxi driver. She could not understand a word that the driver was saying. She motioned to a policeman walking nearby, wanting him to handle the situation. The policeman said, "No, no" and started talking to a man in the gathering crowd. She could not understand why the police officer would not help her. Two police officers with slightly different uniforms than the previous officers arrived at the accident scene. One of them spoke English. He told her that it would be best if she and the taxi driver reached an agreement there rather than going to court.

What is the best thing for Julie to do in this situation?

1. She should immediately call her husband and let him handle the situation.

2. Julie should follow the police officer's advice.

3. She should follow the accident procedures required by Bill's company.

4. She should insist that the police handle the situation.

57   DON'T HIT MY MERCEDES

1. Bill might be of some help, particularly if he can arrive promptly. Otherwise, there is not much that Bill can do to help her from a distance. Please choose again.

2. Even though Turks generally handle traffic accidents without personal injuries in this manner, she, as a foreigner, should have better guidelines. Please choose again.

3. Before starting to drive in Turkey, it is essential to be aware of the exact procedure to follow in case of an accident. Being the foreigner, you must be aware of how to protect yourself in emergency situations. Bill's company should have provided Julie with the company's procedure to follow in this situation. This is the best answer.

4. Being a foreigner, she needs to be aware of what to do in this situation. As in the United States, the police report is only a part of the overall legal situation that needs to be addressed in the case of an accident. Please choose again.

58   CLEAN UP YOUR ACT

One afternoon, Bill and Bryan decided to stroll the main street of Eskişehir. They had heard that the afternoon walk was very pleasant. Along the way they passed several young Turkish workers from the plant. Bill and Bryan then passed some girls in blue school uniforms who were talking and laughing. They could not take their eyes off the group of girls and decided to talk to them. After walking with the girls for a few minutes they were stopped by several young Turks and were told to clean up their act or else...

Why were the Turks upset?

1. They were envious of Bill and Bryan for their courage in talking to the girls.

2. The Americans were approached by the protective brothers of the girls.

3. The Turks thought that the girls were too young to be approached by men.

4. Women should not be approached in public by men who are strangers.

58   CLEAN UP YOUR ACT

1. This is not a correct answer. Please choose again.

2. There is nothing in the episode to indicate that the men are the girls' brothers. Please choose again.

3. In Turkish culture, young girls are protected from strangers. There is, however, a better answer. Please choose again.

4. In places outside of large urban areas such as İstanbul, Ankara, and İzmir, separation of the sexes is more pronounced. It is improper for a man to approach a woman whom he does not know. In general, Turkish culture is protective of women. In the episode this protectionism was accentuated by the fact that Bill and Bryan were Americans. This is the best answer.

59   SULTANAHMET SQUARE

Bill and John were on their way to Europe to spend their summer
traveling together. Having seen many of the Western European
countries before, they decided to see more exotic countries like
Yugoslavia, Greece and Turkey. They started taking trains from
country to country.

After getting off the train in İstanbul, they visited Sultanahmet
Square, a famous gathering place in İstanbul for young tourists.
The Sultanahmet area contains most of the youth hostels and
many cheap restaurants. The next day Bill took a bus tour of the
city while John returned to Sultanahmet to see the Swedish girl,
Anna, he had met the day before.

Anna took John to a restaurant where they had breakfast. Later,
while they were watching a Spanish student playing guitar in the
Square, Anna took a small bag of marijuana from her purse and
unsuccessfully tried to roll a joint. John took the bag and finished
rolling the cigarette. Before he even had time to light it, several
policemen came and grabbed him and Anna. Finding the rest
of the marijuana in John's pocket, they arrested them. After
questioning Anna they set her free, but John was scheduled to
appear in court.

What is the most important issue to know here?

1. Use and possession of drugs carry severe criminal penalties in
   Turkey.

2. Americans are highly suspect for drug use and are generally
   disliked by the police.

3. The police often act as if they were above the law in dealing
   with foreigners.

4. The Turkish public strongly condemns drug use.

59   SULTANAHMET SQUARE

1. Laws and the cultural views of drug use vary from country to country, and it is essential to know that it is not tolerated either culturally or legally in Turkey. If caught, the legal punishment is severe. Turkish law penalizes drug traffickers as severely as murderers. This is the correct answer.

2. Although it is often foreign visitors who are arrested for drug use, this is because there are strong cultural sanctions against drug use among Turks. Some Turks believe that young American and European tourists come to Turkey in part for illicit drug activity, and they might therefore be more suspect. However, there is a better answer. Please choose again.

3. This impression is usually developed from movies and is generally incorrect. Please choose again.

4. This is true because drug use is seen as a showing lack of respect for oneself by misusing one's body. Please choose again for a more complete answer.

D. Traveling

**Don't stop now.
There is more to enjoy!**

60   TAXI ADVENTURE

Osman invited his college friends from the United States, Fred, Susan, and Anita, to visit him in Turkey during the summer. Consequently, they included Turkey in their summer vacation plans for Europe.

In August, Fred, Susan and Anita took a plane from Munich to İstanbul. Osman met them at Atatürk Airport. They took a taxi from the airport to the motel at which Osman had made reservations. On the way, it seemed to the Americans that the taxi driver was driving too fast and recklessly. They also noticed that some other drivers were driving as fast and changing lanes without signaling. Fred, Susan and Anita were scared to death. Fred wanted to tell the driver to stop and let him out of the car, but was afraid of hurting Osman's feelings.

What was the best thing Fred could do under the circumstances from a cultural standpoint?

1. The taxi driver is a professional and accustomed to driving in Turkey; Fred should remain silent and rely upon the driver's expertise.

2. To avoid offending the driver or Osman, Fred should tactfully express his concerns first to Osman.

3. Fred should openly express his concerns; Osman and the driver would be understanding of his request.

4. Fred should ask the two women, Susan and Anita, to request the driver to slow down.

60   TAXI ADVENTURE

1. This situation was written to make you aware that the first encounter with a taxi ride can be very unsettling. The "rules of the road" are different in Turkey, and it takes a while to get used to them. In the situation described, trying to accept the situation as it is may be an alternative, but it fails to address a significant cultural point. Please choose again.

2. Fred may feel better by voicing his concern to Osman. Osman could better judge if the driver's actions are unsafe, and would be better equipped to tactfully request that the driver slow down. This is probably the best answer from a cultural perspective. However, cultural aspects aside, one must otherwise take any actions necessary under the circumstances to avoid potential harm.

3. This is a plausible answer. If Fred feels that it will help to voice his objection, he could do so, but there is a better alternative from a cultural standpoint. Please choose again.

4. Using the women to voice his concern would probably be somewhat effective, but might offend Osman because he is the host. Please choose again.

61   PICTURE THIS

Bob and his family were living in İstanbul where Bob was a visiting professor. On a trip to Ankara, they walked up the hill to the Citadel (an old fortress). They noticed a German tour group nearby. A group of Turkish peasant women living in the area were drawing water at a public fountain. One of the German tourists took a picture of the women. The women became very angry, and one of them threw a pail of water toward him.

Can you explain the women's actions?

1. It is improper for strangers to photograph women in Turkey.

2. Germans are not particularly welcome in Turkey.

3. Some people believe that being photographed steals your soul.

4. The women felt that the photographer was being intrusive.

61   PICTURE THIS

1. It is true that women are more protected in Turkey, but there is a better answer. Please choose again.

2. Although there are some unresolved issues between Germany and Turkey concerning the situation of Turkish workers in Germany, Germans are probably as welcome in Turkey as other European visitors. Please choose again.

3. Some people, especially in the villages of eastern Turkey, may still believe this, but there is a better answer. Please choose again.

4. It is always courteous to ask permission before taking someone's picture. Some people might object for various reasons. This is probably the best answer.

62   IS THAT FAIR?

During their stay in Turkey the Waltons wanted to take a week's vacation in the Aegean-Mediterranean coastal regions of Turkey. They had heard about the beautiful beaches and the many historical sites. They had also heard that driving might not be easy for a foreigner, so they decided to take a taxi wherever they went for sightseeing.

The day before their departure, they asked the hotel manager to arrange a taxi for them for the following morning to go to Efes (Ephesus) from İzmir. They had tickets for the Russian Bolshoi Ballet's performance that night at the Efes Art Festival. The taxi driver picked them up at their hotel early in the morning. When they arrived at Efes a little before noon, Mr. Walton asked the driver how much they owed. The fare that the driver requested was three times as much as what the hotel manager had told them to pay.

Why did the driver ask for that much money?

1. The manager did not correctly estimate the fare.

2. The hotel manager's estimate did not account for the frequent sightseeing stops.

3. The taxi driver was trying to take advantage of the American tourists.

4. The Waltons had not bargained with the driver before starting the trip.

62   IS THAT FAIR?

1. It is unlikely the manager would have quoted a fare that was so grossly incorrect. Please choose again.

2. There is no mention of frequent sightseeing stops in the incident. Please choose again.

3. As in any country, some local people may try to take advantage of a tourist. There is, however, a better answer. Please choose again.

4. Bargaining comes into play for a trip that is not covered by the taxi meter. The meter generally would apply to trips within a city, but bargaining would usually be required for all other trips. Coming to a definite agreement at the beginning of a trip can help avert situations like this one. The driver probably assumed that money was not an issue for them, due to their lack of bargaining. This is the best answer.

63   ANITKABİR (ATATÜRK'S MAUSOLEUM)

Wayne and his family were living in İstanbul where Wayne was a Fulbright scholar at Bosphorus University. They took a trip to Ankara and visited Atatürk's Mausoleum. A martial tune was playing, and other visitors were standing still. Anxious to see everything, Wayne walked on ahead. With his hands in his pockets, he leisurely strolled up to Atatürk's tomb. One of the soldiers guarding the tomb rushed up to Wayne and was most upset, speaking very rapidly in Turkish. Wayne, who could not understand Turkish, became frightened and did not know what to do. Luckily an older Turkish officer who knew English approached Wayne and the guard. Relieved to find an English speaking person, Wayne explained to him that he, in no way, meant to do anything wrong. The Turkish officer spoke with the guard, and Wayne was allowed to leave. Wayne felt shaken and did not understand what the disturbance was all about.

What is the most probable cause for the guard's reaction?

1. The guard considered Wayne's demeanor to be disrespectful.

2. The guard thought that Wayne looked suspicious.

3. Wayne had a camera around his neck, and cameras are not allowed in Atatürk's Mausoleum.

4. Wayne was dressed too casually for such an important place.

63   ANITKABİR (ATATÜRK'S MAUSOLEUM)

1. Showing respect to the memory of Atatürk, as well as standing at attention when the anthem is being played, are expected. Having his hands in his pockets, indicated that Wayne was being very casual about visiting the tomb. He should have also noticed that everyone was standing still, while a song was being played, and done the same. It was probably İstiklal Marşı, the Turkish national anthem, but even if he did not know the music, as a foreigner it is important to always be aware of what others are doing. This is the best answer.

2. Although Wayne had his hands in his pockets, it is unlikely that a university professor would look like a security threat. Please choose again.

3. There is nothing to indicate that Wayne had a camera around his neck. Please choose again.

4. We do not know what Wayne was wearing that day, but being in decent dress is important in public, especially at an important place like Atatürk's tomb. In general, Americans traveling in Turkey should dress more conservatively than in the United States. Shorts, brief tops and colorful casual dress probably would not be appropriate here since such dress might be considered disrespectful to Atatürk's memory. There is, however, a better answer, please choose again.

64   TRIP TO EFES

Jack Adams was proud of being in Turkey to transfer American know-how. He was very interested in historical places and considered himself lucky to have been assigned to Turkey. One weekend he decided to visit Efes (Ephesus) on the Aegean coast of Turkey by bus. Along the way the bus stopped at a roadside restaurant so that the passengers could have lunch. After lunch he went to the restroom and was surprised to be asked by the attendant to put some money in a dish upon leaving the facilities.

Back on the bus, he started talking to the young Turkish man sitting next to him. Jack told him that he really liked Turkey, especially historical places, and that he was working on a joint Turkish-American defense project in Ankara. They had a good conversation going and Jack started talking about how well the project was proceeding and how the Turkish company welcomed the American technology. After some small talk, the conversation died down and the Turkish man turned away and started talking with another Turk across the aisle.

Why did the conversation cease?

1. Being from different cultures Jack and the Turk ran out of things to talk about.

2. Jack and the young Turk felt a generation gap.

3. The Turk did not like the fact that Jack was working on a defense project.

4. The Turk understood Jack to imply that Turkey is a backward country.

64   TRIP TO EFES

1. It is difficult to find topics common to both Americans and Turks when embarking on a casual conversation. A common culture provides much of the basis for everyday conversations. The somewhat abrupt end to the conversation, however, indicates a cultural point. Please choose again.

2. Jack's age is not stated, and he could be a young man. The relatively sudden end to a good conversation suggests another reason. Please choose again.

3. This could be correct, since some Turks may view the American presence in Turkey largely a matter of self-interest for the United States. There is, however, another point. Please choose again.

4. Jack made a mistake by implying that the Turkish company needs American technology. Turks are very proud of their country's accomplishments and resent characterization as a nation requiring the importation of foreign technology. Jack could have described his work in terms of joint cooperation between members of NATO. This is the best answer.

65   TRAIN TRIP TO LAKE VAN

Brad Fisher and his family decided to visit the Lake Van region in eastern Turkey by train. The night before their trip, Brad, his wife Dorothy, and their two children Jerry and Sally enthusiastically packed for their adventure.

The Fishers boarded the train early in the morning at Haydarpaşa Train Station. The children excitedly pressed their noses against the window, watching the outskirts of İstanbul pass by. About two hours later the train pulled into İzmit. An elderly Turkish couple entered their compartment and motioned toward the vacant seats. Jim politely nodded for them to sit down. The old couple acted very friendly, smiling and showing affection toward the children. Later, the Turkish man took out a pack of Samsun cigarettes and offered one, first to Dorothy and then to Brad. Dorothy politely declined but Brad accepted, and the Turkish gentleman also took one for himself. Before Brad could reach for his lighter, the Turkish man offered Brad a light and then lit his own.

Around lunch time, the Turkish couple started to unpack a basket of food that they had brought with them. The old lady arranged the food on a cloth and motioned to the Fishers to join in. Brad and Dorothy instead sheepishly excused themselves and directed the children toward the dining car.

Why do you think the elderly couple acted in this manner?

1. Jerry and Sally reminded them of their grandchildren.

2. The elderly couple thought that the Fishers would have their own food that they would contribute to the joint meal.

3. The Turkish couple was expecting a reciprocating gift.

4. The Turks were showing their hospitality.

65   TRAIN TRIP TO LAKE VAN

1. This could be true, since Turks highly value children and the family in general, but there is another point. Please choose again.

2. The elderly couple would probably share their food without expecting anything in return. Please choose again.

3. This is not likely to be true. Please choose again.

4. Turks are a very hospitable people and share whatever they have. It is always polite to offer food, cigarettes, etc. to others around you before helping yourself. This is the best answer.

66   UNDERWATER ADVENTURE

Jill and her husband were vacationing on the Mediterranean coast
of Turkey. They wanted to explore some underwater ruins that
they had heard about from some American tourists. Diving was
their hobby, and they owned their own equipment. With a young
boy from the nearby village acting as a guide, they searched the
waters for almost a day. Suddenly the guide shouted, pointing to
a shiny object under the surface. Jill quickly dove to the spot and
came to the surface with a partially encrusted coin.

When they returned to their home in Ankara, Jill proudly showed
her find to their Turkish friends Hakkı and Nimet. The Turks
glanced at each other and tried to change the conversation.

Why did Jill's Turkish friends behave in this manner?

1. They felt that it was inappropriate for Jill and her husband to
   take a part of Turkey's historic richness.

2. The Turks feared that Jill and her husband were breaking the
   law.

3. The Turkish friends were resentful that two foreigners had
   found something quite valuable.

4. The Turks thought that Jill was being silly for making a big
   deal out of an obvious replica of an old coin.

66   UNDERWATER ADVENTURE

1. In the past, many historic treasures of Turkey were illegally removed and taken to other countries. Therefore, Turks feel protective as well as proud of their historic heritage. Please choose again for a more important point.

2. It is against the law to keep and/or remove antiquities from Turkey, a law which carries heavy penalties. The law has broad application, and all visitors to Turkey should acquaint themselves with its provisions. This is the best answer.

3. Good friends would not feel this way. Please choose again.

4. Replicas of old coins have been known to be made by local youths at tourist areas, for sale to eager tourists. Since the young boy spotted the coin, it is a possibility to check out. If it is not real, you can keep it. If it is authentic, however, check the laws governing antiquities in Turkey. See #2 above.

E. Adjustment

You are almost finished.
Congratulations!

67   V.I.P. TREATMENT

Bill was transferred to Ankara as the chief financial officer for the start-up phase of a new project. Once he accepted the position, his company started treating him like a V.I.P. The first step was to send Bill to Turkey for a week-long get-acquainted trip. Upon his return home he was provided with a two week Turkish language and cultural training program. The company moved his family's household goods to Turkey, allowed him a generous housing allowance, provided him with a car, and paid for the schooling of his children Joel and Lija, ages 13 and 8.

After arriving in Turkey, Bill was pleased that his job was going well. However, problems started appearing at home. His wife was often upset and depressed when he got home from work. She had been an interior designer in the United States and missed her profession. She wondered if any of her clients would remember her when she returned to the States. She also felt that having a maid around invaded her privacy, yet she did not want to spend her days cooking and cleaning. The children were missing their friends back home and were not doing well at their new schools.

What is the most probable reason for the problems that Bill's family is experiencing?

1. Bill and his family are experiencing cultural adjustment problems.

2. Bill's family was not adequately prepared for the cultural difficulties awaiting them in Turkey.

3. The problems stem from the unhappiness of Bill's career-oriented wife.

4. The children were having problems at school due to the language barrier.

67   V.I.P TREATMENT

1. This is a correct answer except that Bill is not suffering any adjustment problems, just his family. Please choose again.

2. A very common mistake some companies make is to pay most of their attention to the employee who has accepted a position abroad, and ignore his/her family. This episode is an example of what can happen once the family is abroad. The husband was given many opportunities to see, as well as learn about, Turkey. His family received none of this and is possibly having a difficult time adjusting because of this. This is the best choice.

3. Career-oriented wives face a great challenge in leaving their careers behind for the sake of the husband's career. Usually they cannot work abroad and must deal with their feelings of being relegated to a non-working woman status. The children's adaptation has also been found to depend on the mother's adjustment. There is a more important point, however, please choose again.

4. American children in Turkey would most likely be attending an English speaking school, so that they would not be dealing with a language barrier. Please choose again.

68   A TURKISH BATH HEALS ANYTHING!

Jack was sent to Ankara to train some Turks. He initially adjusted quite well. As time went on, however, he became increasingly intimidated by the educational background of the Turks he was training. In the United States, not having a college degree had never bothered him, but now it did.

He was also homesick for his fiancée who worked as a real estate agent in the United States, but at the same time, felt attracted to one of the single Turkish women at work. She was part of the group he usually had tea with, and he felt captivated by her innocence and warmth.

Jack started feeling ill and complained to one of his Turkish friends about stomach aches, lower back pains, and headaches. His friend suggested that a Turkish hamam (bath) might help him feel better. Jack was ready to try anything; he spent the next Saturday morning at the nearby hamam, soaking in the hot pool and enjoying the steam room. On the way home he stopped at the local pharmacy, and bought some over-the-counter pills suggested by the pharmacist. Jack's symptoms persisted, and he finally went to the base doctor. The doctor prescribed some more pills, but the problems still did not go away.

What is causing Jack's problems?

1. Jack is a hypochondriac and looking for an impossible cure.

2. Jack has never before suffered the pressure of managing workers better educated than he.

3. Jack is questioning the American values that made him love his American fiancée.

4. Jack's symptoms may stem from his cultural adjustment.

68   A TURKISH BATH HEALS ANYTHING!

1. There is nothing in the incident to indicate that this was his pattern of behavior. Please choose again.

2. Some Americans find the education level of the Turks they are training and working with to be higher than their own. This can cause feelings of inadequacy and questioning of self-worth, considering the cultural differences that have to be dealt with as well. This does not have to be an issue if Jack is competent in his job as well as open to establishing good relationships with the Turks with whom he is working. There is a better point. Please choose again.

3. A common challenge of living abroad is that one begins to question the values one has always held. Our values are mainly unconscious until we come up against those of another culture, and are challenged to look at ourselves in a new light. Jack may very well be questioning his relationship with his fiancée by feeling the attraction to the Turkish woman, but there is a more important point. Please choose again.

4. Although partial explanations have been offered in the previous responses, we cannot tell what is really bothering Jack, since he is looking for a cure only for his physical ailments. They may not go away because they could be symptoms of cultural adjustment. If so, Jack needs to address the root of the problem. Jack's insecurity about work, his homesickness, and his feelings for the Turkish woman may all be part of his cultural adjustment process. This is the best answer.

69   A GOOD CAREER MOVE

Richard and Nancy had been in Turkey for five months. Their assignment was for two years, and this was a good career move for Richard. Their initial excitement of living in İzmit and of the good financial package faded slowly. They were starting to criticize each other, finding fault with otherwise insignificant shortcomings. Nancy noticed that Richard had begun to complain about his Turkish co-workers and his job in general. In addition, he was slowly increasing the number of beers he was having after work to where he was up to six a night by the fifth month. He had seldom touched alcohol in the United States.

Nancy's repeated attempts to help Richard were of no avail. At the same time, she started venturing out less and less, and her interest in Richard began to wane. Instead, she occupied most of her time cleaning the ever present dust and dirt from the apartment. She was feeling isolated, even secretly feeling at times that she was going crazy.

What is happening to Nancy?

1. Nancy feels that she is helpless in dealing with her husband's adjustment problems.

2. Nancy is depressed because she is afraid that Richard is becoming an alcoholic.

3. Nancy is increasingly worried that their marriage is falling apart.

4. Nancy and her husband are experiencing cultural transition problems.

69   **A GOOD CAREER MOVE**

1. This is plausible, because Richard is not responding to her attempts to help him. There is a better explanation, however, please choose again.

2. Many Americans end up with alcohol problems once they are abroad. It is a common way for people to deal with the stress of overseas living. There is a better answer, however, please choose again.

3. Since they are fighting more frequently and she is losing interest in her husband, this is a plausible choice. The stress of cultural adjustment has been known to break up marriages. However, there is a better choice. Please choose again.

4. This incident points out several ways that people experience what is commonly termed "culture shock." The stress of adapting to a new culture manifests itself in different ways for different people, and it is important to be aware of this fact. This is the best answer.

70   OTHER PEOPLE'S KIDS

Jim and Mary and their children, Chris age two and Molly age four, had been in Turkey for six months. Mary had adjusted well and enjoyed having a full-time maid, Kadriye, to help with the housework, cooking and children. Kadriye would bring her five year old daughter with her from time to time. Mary was pleased that the children were getting to know each other. Before coming to Turkey, Mary had decided that she would do whatever it took to facilitate a good and quick adjustment to Turkey for the family, so that Jim could concentrate on his job. As the months passed, however, Mary started feeling increasingly stressed and emotional. One day, Kadriye's daughter accidentally dropped a crystal vase on the marble entry floor. Mary was so startled by the sound that she jumped up and screamed at the little girl and burst into tears muttering, "I cannot take any more."

What is the most probable cause of Mary's outburst?

1. Mary can no longer tolerate the lack of privacy.

2. Mary is apparently suffering from cross-cultural adjustment difficulties.

3. Mary is upset because the child broke her favorite vase.

4. Mary used this as an excuse to vent her displeasure with Kadriye's performance.

70   OTHER PEOPLE'S KIDS

1. Many Americans may have never had a maid before. Since Americans value privacy, having another person in the house can be a difficult adjustment. This incident indicates, however, that Mary enjoyed having a full-time maid. Please choose again.

2. This situation suggests culture shock as the best choice. In her determination to help her family adjust, Mary was putting her own needs last. She finally released her pent up emotions at the little girl. The non-working wife probably has the most difficult adjustment challenge, because she does not have the structure of a job, and the whole family looks to her for support. She must be aware of her own needs, and meet them as much as possible.

3. This can be true although the incident does not indicate that it was her favorite vase. Please choose again.

4. Sometimes it is easier to deal with a problem indirectly, such as suggested here, but nothing indicates that Mary was not happy with Kadriye's work. Please choose again.

71   A NEW DIRECTION IN LIFE

Don and Jane were in their mid-forties. Don had been very successful with his company but felt unchallenged and restless. He and Jane were not as close as they used to be. Their children had been their mutual focus, and now they were gone. Jane felt unneeded and with no direction for her life.

One day Don was asked by his company to be part of a management team of the business venture in İzmir. He and Jane felt this was just what they needed to make their life exciting. They eagerly read all they could about Turkey, bought some Turkish language tapes, and made a point of finding some Turkish students to learn about the culture.

After the initial excitement of the first couple of months wore off, they started having a hard time adjusting to İzmir. The other Americans assured them that it was normal to go through this adjustment phase and that everything would be fine. They did start to adapt better to the culture with time, but their relationship grew increasingly strained. They eventually found it impossible to relate to each other and decided to return to the United States after only six months in Turkey.

What was probably the main reason for their early return?

1. Don and Jane could not adjust to the new culture.

2. They were homesick for friends and family in the United States.

3. The job in Turkey was not the challenging position that Don had been seeking.

4. Don and Jane's previous marital problems resurfaced in Turkey.

71   A NEW DIRECTION IN LIFE

1. This is not indicated in the episode. They did have difficulty at first, but adapted better after that. Please choose again.

2. Homesickness is common during the adjustment phase and could be the case here. There is, however, a better answer. Please choose again.

3. The episode does not suggest this. Please choose again.

4. Don and Jane were hoping that going overseas would revitalize their marriage. This is not usually the cure; quite the opposite often happens. With the added stress of adjusting to a new culture, marriages can fall apart. It is best to have a good relationship before deciding to live abroad, since mutual support is very important during the adjustment cycle.

72   TONY'S TALES

Tony had just returned from a three-year project in Turkey. He had greatly enjoyed Turkey and felt that he had learned much about himself and different ways of living. Before leaving Turkey he had pictured how wonderful his return would be and the hours he would spend telling friends and family about his experiences, not to mention showing them his wonderful slides. Upon returning, he was crushed to find that after the first 15 minutes of listening to his tales of life in Turkey, everyone changed the subject to what they had been doing in the United States. He felt very much alone, isolated and uncared-for. He began wishing that he had not left Turkey.

What is happening in this situation?

1. To his friends Tony's memories were just interesting stories, but to him they represented three years of his life.

2. Tony's friends did not like Turkey.

3. Tony's friends are jealous of Tony's experiences in Turkey.

4. Tony is being overly sensitive to his friends' reactions.

72   TONY'S TALES

1. Living abroad is a very meaningful experience, one that is never forgotten, but may cause problems when friends do not share the intensity of interest. Returning home is not expected to create adjustment difficulties, but often it does. This is the best answer.

2. There is nothing to indicate this in the incident. Please choose again.

3. This could be true of his friends who have never traveled and wished they could. There is a better answer, however, please choose again.

4. This could be true, because it is important to be able to share one's experiences when returning home. There is, however, a more important point to be understood. Please choose again.

73   HOME IS WHERE THE HEART IS

John and Darlene had been back home in California for three months. They felt confused because they missed Turkey and spent much of their time fondly recalling their time in Ankara. They had disliked many things while there, such as the smoggy air in the winter, the water shortages in the summer, and the many problems at work, yet they longed to be there. While in Ankara, on the other hand, they had longed for and talked incessantly about San Diego: how beautiful it was, the ocean nearby, the Safeway just down the street. Yet, somehow, those things turned out not to be so important once they returned, and life in Turkey had become so strongly their focus of attention. Two years in Ankara had left a feeling of "home" in them that they did not realize was there until now.

Can you help John and Darlene understand what they are experiencing?

1. As with many things, absence makes the heart grow fonder.

2. Now that they have lived in both places, John and Darlene prefer Ankara.

3. John and Darlene are malcontents and would not be happy anywhere.

4. They are undergoing a period of readjustment, and their values and perceptions are in flux.

73   HOME IS WHERE THE HEART IS

1. This is partially true because people tend to remember the positive experiences and downplay the rest. Please choose again.

2. This is not likely to be true, since they have just been back in the United States for three months. Please choose again.

3. There is nothing to indicate this about John and Darlene. Please choose again.

4. Just as there was a period of adjustment when John and Mary arrived in Turkey, there is one upon returning home. Having lived in another culture calls for one's reevaluation of values and perceptions. This takes time and manifests itself differently in everyone. It is helpful to be aware of this and learn about it before returning home. This is the best answer.

BIBLIOGRAPHY

Austin, C.N., ed. *Cross-Cultural Reentry: A Book of Readings.* Abilene, TX: Abilene Christian University Press (1986).

*Baruch, H. "International Transactions Which Violate the Foreign Corrupt Practices Act or Other Criminal Statutes." Reprinted in *Law & Practice of United States Regulation of International Trade,* edited by C.R. Johnson. New York, NY: Oceana Publications, Inc. (1987).

Brislin, R., Cushner, K., Cherrie, C., and Yong, M. *Intercultural Interactions: A Practical Guide.* Beverly Hills, CA: Sage Publications (1986).

*Fadiman, J.A. "A Traveler's Guide to Gifts and Bribes." *Harvard Business Review.* 64:122–136, July-August (1986).

Kağıtçıbaşı, Ç, ed. *Sex Roles, Family & Community in Turkey.* Bloomington, IN: Indiana University Press (1982).

Lord Kinross. *Atatürk.* New York, NY: William Morrow and Co. (1965).

Kohls, L.R. *Survival Kit for Overseas Living* (2nd ed.). Yarmouth, ME: Intercultural Press, Inc. (1984).

Lewis, B. *The Emergence of Modern Turkey.* New York, NY: Oxford University Press (1961).

Muallimoğlu, N. *The Wit and Wisdom of Nasreddin Hodja.* New York, NY: Cynthia Parzych Publishing, Inc. (1986).

* Perkins, S.C. "Bibliography on the Foreign Corrupt Practices Act of 1977." *Western State University Law Review.* 14:491–521 (1987).

---

*These materials do not reflect the changes introduced by the Foreign Corrupt Practices Act Amendments of 1988 enacted as part of the Trade and Competitiveness Act of 1988.

Stewart, E.C. *American Cultural Patterns: A Cross-Cultural Perspective* Yarmouth, ME: Intercultural Press, Inc. (1972).

Triandis, H.C., Brislin, R., and Hui, C.H. "Cross-Cultural Training Across the Individualism-Collectivism Divide." *International Journal of Intercultural Relations.* 12:269–289 (1988).

Triandis, H.C. "A Theoretical Framework for the More Efficient Construction of Culture Assimilators." *International Journal of Intercultural Relations.* 8:301–330 (1984).

Turkish Embassy Culture and Tourism Counselor's Office. "Turkey in Brief" Washington, D.C. (1986).

Ural, E. *Turkish Law for Foreigners.* Ankara, Turkey (1988).

Walker, K. B. *A Treasury of Turkish Folktales for Children.* Hamden, CT: Linnet Books, The Shoe String Press (1988).

Walker, K. B. *Turkish Games for Health and Recreation.* Lubbock, TX: Texas Tech Press (1983).

Weiker, W. *The Modernization of Turkey, from Atatürk to the Present Day.* New York, NY: Holmes and Meier Publishers, Inc. (1981).

Reader Suggestions

Dear Reader:

We hope you enjoyed reading this book. In our continuing process of improving it, we solicit your general comments about the book and any of your personal experiences which could be the basis of new cultural episodes for future editions. As you reflect on your experiences be especially aware of incidents that repeat themselves, because they may indicate cultural differences.

Any of your comments or experiences will be greatly appreciated. Please send them to:

International Concepts, Ltd.
5311 Holmes Place
Boulder, CO 80303-1243
U.S.A.

Thank You!

Unconditional Return Policy!

If you are not satisfied with this book for any reason return it undamaged within ten days for a full refund of the purchase price.

Order Form

MAIL ORDERS TO:

    International Concepts, Ltd.
    5311 Holmes Place
    Boulder, CO 80303-1243
    U.S.A.
    (303) 442-8144

Please send me _____ copies @ $19.95 ea. $ _____

Colorado residents add 60¢ sales tax for
  each book ordered .... _____

Shipping and handling .... _____
(**SURFACE:** Add $1.50 for the first book and $1.00 for each
additional book. **UPS 2ND DAY AIR:** Add $3.00 for the first
book and $2.00 for each additional book. Charges for orders
outside the U.S. provided upon request.)

TOTAL PAYMENT ....$_____

_____ Check or money order enclosed
_____ Please charge my credit card:
                  _____ Mastercard _____Visa

Phone #: (   ) _____

Credit card #: _____
Credit card expires: _____

Signature: _____

Name: _____

Address: _____

City/State/Zip: _____

Please make checks payable to **International Concepts, Ltd.**
All checks must be in U.S. funds and drawn on a U.S. bank
or a U.S. branch of a foreign bank.

Thank you for your order!

Unconditional Return Policy!

If you are not satisfied with this book for any reason return it undamaged within ten days for a full refund of the purchase price.

Order Form

<u>MAIL ORDERS TO:</u>

International Concepts, Ltd.
5311 Holmes Place
Boulder, CO 80303-1243
U.S.A.
(303) 442-8144

Please send me ____ copies @ $19.95 ea. $ _____

Colorado residents add 60¢ sales tax for
  each book ordered .... _____

Shipping and handling .... _____
(**SURFACE:** Add $1.50 for the first book and $1.00 for each
additional book. **UPS 2ND DAY AIR:** Add $3.00 for the first
book and $2.00 for each additional book. Charges for orders
outside the U.S. provided upon request.)

TOTAL PAYMENT ....$_____

____ Check or money order enclosed
____ Please charge my credit card:
                    _____ Mastercard _____ Visa

Phone #: (   ) _____

Credit card #: ⬚⬚⬚⬚⬚⬚⬚⬚⬚⬚⬚⬚⬚⬚⬚⬚⬚
Credit card expires: _____

Signature: _____

Name: _____

Address: _____
         _____
City/State/Zip: _____

Please make checks payable to **International Concepts, Ltd.**
All checks must be in U.S. funds and drawn on a U.S. bank
or a U.S. branch of a foreign bank.

Thank you for your order!